GORDON GREENIDGE
The Man In The Middle

GORDON GREENIDGE

The Man In The Middle

Gordon Greenidge with
Patrick Symes

DAVID & CHARLES
Newton Abbot   London   North Pomfret (Vt)

Library of Congress Catalog Card Number
80—65424

ISBN 0 7153 8044 3

Typeset by ABM Typographics Ltd, Hull
Printed in Great Britain
by Redwood Burn, Ltd, Trowbridge & Esher
for David & Charles (Publishers) Limited
Brunel House Newton Abbot Devon

Published in the United States of America
by David & Charles Inc
North Pomfret   Vermont 05053   USA

Contents

1 Barbadian Background

The little West Indian island of Barbados has probably produced more cricketers per square foot than any other place in the world. Cricket is a way of life in Barbados and it was there, during the first fourteen years of my life, that I came to learn the rudiments of a game which has been the corner stone of my entire existence. Yet, having said that, it was never my intention to be cricketer and it was not until long after I had arrived in England and joined the Hampshire staff that I realised I had enough ability to make a living from the game and, in the estimations of some, become one of its greatest contemporary exponents.

It may surprise some people to learn that when I first left school I seriously considered becoming a preacher. At that time I used to go to church three times a week and when one of my best friends joined the Church I gave the matter much thought before deciding against the idea. Certainly as a seventeen year old, it seemed a much more feasible career than playing cricket and there were those connected with the Church who did their best to help me change my mind. By that time I was living in Reading, Berkshire, a provincial English town, some 40 miles from London and choking with light industry and with rows of terraced homes every bit as repressive as those in the north of the country.

Reading's drabness was a far cry from the village of Black Bess in St Peter, Barbados where I first saw the light of day on 1 May 1951. My mother was not married and until I was about twelve I was brought up as Cuthbert Gordon Lavine. It was not until my mother came to England and married a Barbadian that I took his name of Greenidge.

My uncles played cricket on a little pitch hewn from rough

ground above our home and it was there that I came to first understand a game which has since dominated my life. They regarded me as something of a pest because I always wanted to bat and in order to do so I used to stand on the ball in the long grass until they gave in. Thank goodness I do not have to go to such extreme lengths nowadays. At St Peter Boys' School we played on a proper grass wicket where, as a ten year old, I was in the school team with boys three or more years older. Barbados may seem like a paradise with the constant warm sunshine, the sand and the cane fields but economically it is far from wealthy and my mother, a qualified seamstress, was forced to follow a well-worn trail to the British Isles in search of regular work and decent wages.

From the age of eight I was brought up by my grandmother and, since there was no father to contribute, times were hard. My mother went to London on her own and while working in a bakery in London, sent back money when she could. Eventually she met and married the man I now call my father and when they settled in Reading they sent for me to come and live with them. To a fourteen year old, raised on a dreamy little island like Barbados, it was like setting feet in hell. We lived in a terrace house with no back garden and none of the wide open spaces I had been used to. It all seemed so cold and miserable and after enrolling at Alfred Sutton's Secondary School, my problems were only just beginning. Not only were the methods of education so different but also I collided head on with something I had heard about yet had never fully considered: racial prejudice.

In Barbados we had heard tales of the anti-black feeling in Britain but never did I expect to encounter the depth of hatred when as a bewildered teenager I first went to an English school. 'Black bastard' was the least of the taunts and before long I became enmeshed in bitter playground scraps. Perhaps I should not have risen to the bait but I did and the penalty was more than one caning from the headmaster to add injury to insult. One of the major problems was the way I spoke. My thick West Indian accent became an easy target and I found it difficult to believe that others could not understand what I was saying. Now my accent betrays

8

my years in Britain but it was some time before I learned that I had to speak more slowly. Reading is full of West Indians attracted by the demand for semi-skilled labour but although there were plenty at my school, none of them came to my aid. This, too, I found strange. Some had been through the same torment as myself and did not want to fight my battles for me but there were others who simply took no interest. This, I was to discover, was because they came from other West Indian islands—Trinidad, Jamaica, Antigua —and they regarded me every bit as foreign as the white Englishmen in whose country they were now living. Indeed to get a West Indian cricket team together is something of a minor miracle because inter-island rivalry is intense and geographically they are far apart in many cases. Many times I felt obliged to exact revenge for the terrible things they called me and it was not unusual for me to limp home with nose and lips bleeding. I was lonely, bewildered and overwhelmed by the sheer size of everything. With no older brother and no friends to turn to, my suffering was all the worse.

Coming into the educational system as a fourteen year old, I never came to terms with colossal changes. I was good at woodwork and I enjoyed history and geography but concentration has never been one of my strong points and I left school, like so many West Indians in Britain, without qualification or hope. Sport was a bit different, though. I played some soccer but particularly I enjoyed rugby. After a few games on the wing I moved into the scrum and I may have been small and skinny and the game may have been rough and dangerous but I became quite effective. Curiously, I think I got as much out of those sports as out of cricket and it was some time before I got into the school's cricket team. In 1967 Alfred Sutton's won the Reading Schools Cricket League but I don't remember ever making more than a very ordinary contribution and then only as a batsman because, like now, I did not enjoy bowling. In grey trousers and canvas gym shoes I hardly looked like a potential Test player; my achievements were minor and there was nothing about me to suggest that I would be anything other than a reasonable weekend club player. What's more, I had no ambition to be a cricketer and no one thought I was good enough either. Anyway, somehow I was chosen for the Berkshire Schools side and to this day I really do not know why. I'm not being falsely modest when I say one of the main reasons was because I was a West Indian. The selectors thought that since I was from Barbados I *had* to be good at cricket. It's a bit like saying that everyone from Liverpool is bound to be a good footballer.

Once again, my record for Berkshire Schools was no more than average. I had a good eye for a ball and I liked to hit it hard and often, yet I cannot honestly remember getting many runs. By now I was enjoying the game much more and occasionally it crossed my mind that it would be good way to make a living, although the chances of actually doing so were as remote as ever. My lack of concentration was my undoing and after making good starts to innings, I was out just when I should have been reaping the benefit.

At fifteen, after a torrid and unpleasant year or so at school, I was forced to look for a job and my cricket career, such as it was, went into cold storage. For £12 a week I went to work for Suttons Seeds in Reading, heaving bags of fertiliser from one building to another and stacking peat. It certainly helped build up my shoulders and I would be lying if I did not say that I quite enjoyed it. Out of sheer boredom I worked as much overtime as I could. Literally to kill time I would work until eight o'clock every night since I had no social life to speak of except the Church. I was very lonely and as a shy and retiring boy I prefered to spend my free time at home. Occasionally I would venture to the Top Rank and there was a West Indian club not far away, but as a raw Barbadian I was never made to feel at home when I went there and I was far too nervous to take the initiative. It was about this time that I thought about going into the Church. A Barbadian friend in Reading, Jefferson Atherley took the step and as a member of the choir, it occurred to me as well. I probably saw it as a means of escape. I was struggling to adjust to a new life, my work was getting me nowhere and my social life was non-existent. Salvation through cricket was a long way off.

The following summer I graduated to the Berkshire Bantams

side and by now, 1967, I was starting to take the game far more seriously. I think it was about now that I thought I might try to become a cricketer although how I was supposed to go about it, I was not sure. I find it hard to recall individual matches of my early years. I kept no press cuttings and the only game that is anything other than a blur was the time I scored 135 not out against Wiltshire. As far as I remember, it was my only major score. Time after time I was making an impressive and belligerent start before getting out needlessly.

It was about now that I was discovered and quite how it all happened, I am still far from sure. Arthur Holt was Hampshire's coach then. He was as shrewd a talent-spotter as any in the game and I believe my name came to his attention after some moderate successes with the Bantams. John Arlott, the broadcaster, is also said to have spotted me. If it all sounds a bit vague that's because I really have no idea, even now, exactly how I came to the attention not only of Hampshire but also Warwickshire. Never did it occur to me to write to any county asking for a trial. When the invitations came in from Hampshire and Warwickshire I had not got a clue what to do about them. I remember feeling flattered but also a little apprehensive. You see, since my arrival in England, I had hardly emerged from my little rut in Reading. My entire life was centred then around a 3-mile radius. Nearby towns like Newbury, Oxford and Wokingham might just as well have been on the moon and the thought of going to places like Birmingham and Southampton for trials genuinely scared me.

Birmingham really is not that far away from Reading but it sounded big and unfamiliar and to an unworldly sixteen year old, the prospect was too much. Ironically I have always enjoyed playing at Edgbaston and I can honestly say that of all the grounds in the world, Edgbaston is my favourite. I always seem to get runs there and who knows how successful I would have been if I had joined them instead of Hampshire. If Birmingham had been closer to my home, I might well have done just that. Southampton sounded nicer and, more to the point, nearer, and it was to the County Ground, home of Hampshire, that I sent back a letter

11

accepting their invitation for a trial in the nets. John Arlott tells the tale of how I had no money to come to Southampton and that he reimbursed my schoolmaster the £4 for my fare. I must say I do not remember this, though that's not to say it is not true. Anyway, my instructions were to board a train at Reading and change at Basingstoke to catch the main London to Southampton train. Full of trepidation I managed this complicated manoeuvre and as the train rattled through the Hampshire countryside I think I would have given anything for the chance to turn back. Not unnaturally, I was a little worried about what I would be required to do, how I would shape up, like all trialists, hoping that my true ability would show through. It all seemed so strange because I was by no means a cricket fanatic. I had no cricketing idol and I doubt whether I could have named any of the Hampshire players of that time. Yet here I was on my way to Southampton with the chances of becoming a cricketer suddenly a very real prospect.

I believe it was Mr Holt who met me at Southampton Station and I was almost trembling with nerves when we reached the ground and the indoor nets. Some of the younger second-team players and one or two more senior ones were detailed to bowl at me and I remember thinking how often I would have been out had a proper match been in progress. People who were obviously important huddled together to discuss me and my somewhat limited success in the nets. I must have done enough to encourage the belief that I had some talent because the secretary, Desmond Eagar, asked me if I would like to spend the rest of the summer with them. I could hardly believe my luck but I was still puzzled and apprehensive. Puzzled as to what others had seen in me and apprehensive because I was not certain that I would ever be good enough to make a county-standard cricketer. For all my fears, I was only too pleased to try my luck and the rest of the season was spent working as a groundstaff boy, picking up paper, cleaning up dressing rooms and helping the groundsmen prepare wickets. Leo Harrison, a Hampshire player for twenty-seven years, was in charge of the second team and on 21 August 1967 I made my second-team debut at Southampton against, with a supreme twist of irony, Warwickshire. We won by 9 wickets but my own contribution had absolutely no affect on the outcome. I held one catch and scored 2 runs batting at number seven. Our team included Harrison himself, Mike Barnard and Henry Horton from Hampshire's championship-winning days of 1961 and several promising youngsters like Richard Lewis, Keith Wheatley and Trevor Jesty, all of whom were a couple of years older and that much more experienced.

There was only one more second-team match that season and I was left out. It rained for most of the summer and I was beginning to despair of a real opportunity to prove that I deserve a contract. With so much rain, few matches I was involved in ever seemed to finish and as the end of August approached I was starting to fear the worst. Then, right at the end of a wet and depressing summer, I was chosen to play for Holt's Colts, as we were popularly known, against the Hampshire Hoggets. Ernie Knights, the Hampshire groundsman, was not too keen on the match taking place for, quite rightly, he felt that untold damage could be done to a very saturated Southampton square. Ernie relented and agreed to allow an hour's batting for each side. This was my chance, and in a match of no great consequence, I scored 95 in 55 minutes and Hampshire quickly offered me a two-year contract. Almost as eagerly, I accepted. Mr Holt, a kind and sympathetic man, and his wife looked after me during that summer and I am indebted to him even now for lending me a pair of pyjamas when the English summer took its traditional turn for the worse. They were far too big for me, but they kept out the cold.

So, I was on my way and, if nothing else, cricket was offering me the chance to escape what was fast becoming a future of no great expectation. Sport has been a means to a better existence for many youngsters from working-class backgrounds and I suppose I am no exception. With an escape route now beckoning, I was determined to make the most of it, and since Hampshire borders Berkshire, I was much happier in the knowledge that everything familiar was not far away—providing I remembered to change at Basingstoke.

Had I not been offered terms by Hampshire I am not sure what I would have done. I think I would have plucked up enough courage to go to Warwickshire for trials, but it never came to that. More likely was a return to Suttons Seeds and a deep reconsideration of my life. The alternatives were not too bright. I was unqualified and unskilled and at the time Hampshire's offer came along I was thinking of going to night school in an effort to give myself more of a choice of job. I have no real idea what I would have studied though two years later with a fellow Barbadian, John Holder, I studied accountancy and book-keeping and have never regretted it. For a few brief moments in the summer of 1967 my gloom was banished, the rains stopped and all I had in my head was cricket and a burning ambition to succeed.

2 Hampshire Apprenticeship

If I thought my problems had ended when I signed Hampshire's contract, I was wrong. They were only just beginning. With all the senior, capped players and the other young hopefuls on the ground-staff, I reported for duty in April 1968, having said farewell finally to Suttons Seeds and these back-breaking bags of fertiliser. No one could have been keener than I in those early days even if, once again, everything was stunningly new to me. For the groundstaff boys under Ernie Knights' guidance there was an endless round of chores before the escape to practice and the nets. There was the waste paper and discarded food, often made wet by the overnight rain, to pick up the day after the conclusion of a first-team match. Pavilions had to be swept and, as in the Army, anything that did not move had to be painted.

It was my efforts at painting which led to my first real brush, if that's the right word, with one of the most senior and respected professionals. 'Butch' White was a fast bowler of the old school. Big, belligerent and bellicose. He took more than a thousand wickets for Hampshire and earned himself a couple of caps at a time when there was plenty of competition for fast-bowling places. Butch was coming to the end of his distinguished career when I first crossed his path and discovered that his bark was every bit as bad as his bite. As the senior professionals trooped off to the nets at Southampton one bright morning, I was outside the pavilion painting the seats green, a task which provided everyone, especially Butch, with huge cause for laughter. As green paint dripped everywhere they were poking fun at me with cries of 'Get on with it, van Gogh' and other such hilarious repartee.

I did not retaliate, but quietly sulked as the seniors went on to the nets. My task done I returned to the dressing rooms to be greeted moments later by the shouts of what seemed like a raging bull. Butch had taken time off for a little rest and, with a cup of tea in his hands, had sat down in the sun . . . on the freshly painted green seats. Of course, when he got up he looked as if he was wearing a convict's uniform—white with green stripes. Obviously he had forgotten the seats were wet, but that did not diminish his anger and I was forced to take to my heels to escape his considerable wrath.

Hampshire had some promising young players on the groundstaff at the time, several of whom have gone on to become the backbone of the first team. Both David Turner and Trevor Jesty emerged as Test candidates at various stages in their careers and in Richard Lewis there was a fine batsman whose results never matched ability. Keith Wheatley was an off-spinner who drifted out of the game at an early age and Alan Castell was one of the first to discover that leg-spinners have to be of exceptional quality to make the grade nowadays. Richie Benaud once described Castell as one of the world's most promising leg-spinners but to get any kind of a game he had to turn to orthodox medium pace before injury finally forced him out. Then there was John Holder, a fast bowler from Barbados who was genuinely quick but too erratic to make much of a lasting mark on the first-class scene. All of us were uncapped and thirsting for the chance to play county cricket. The others were an important year or two older and there were enough calls to the first team to keep them all interested. The county side was a long way off for me in the summer of 1968 and I did little to suggest I was worthy of consideration.

I played in most of the second eleven's matches under Leo Harrison that summer but scored only 227 runs at an average of 22. Indeed only once did I score a half century, an unbeaten 68 against a combined Somerset and Gloucestershre side at Taunton. We finished third in the championship for second teams, having won it the previous year, but my own progress was at best only satisfactory. The Hampshire handbook for 1969 put my achievements in perspective when, in a review of the juniors, my name crops up in the last paragraph: 'Mention should be made of the 17 year old Greenidge who was born in Barbados. He has still much to learn and his fielding leaves much to be desired, but he played a number of useful innings and made good progress during the season.'

It may come as a surprise to learn that my fielding 'left much to be desired'. In truth, I was awful. Now I enjoy a reputation as one of the best fielders in the world game and I like to think I have worked hard enough on that facet of cricket to deserve this kind of recognition. Fielding is a crucial part of any match, but when I first joined the Hampshire staff I hated it—and it showed. Although I was quick and athletic I was such a poor fielder that they used to try and hide me well away from the action and where I could do the least damage. Third man or fine leg were the only places it was thought I was safe, but even then it was no guarantee. Time after time I would be dozing quietly down by the boundary when the ball would roll gently past me—or worse still—through me for four. I could do nothing right in the field and no end of criticism from coaches and colleagues could change my attitude. In my naivety I considered fielding as much a chore as sweeping the changing rooms and, since I did not bowl either, there was only my mediocre batting as a recommendation.

By now I had received my introduction to the place I was to call home for the next two or three years, the Southampton YMCA. Say what you like about these hostels, they are cheap, clean and warm and since my wages were only minimal there was simply no alternative. The YMCAs provide a strange world of their own. Men of all ages use them as a stopping-off point or as a reasonably permanent place to live. Some of the older men were living there, permanently; others had been there seven or eight years with little likelihood of moving on. The first summer was not too bad. I was at the ground early every morning and did not return till late at night, by which time there was little else to do except eat and sleep. But in the winter it was a different and depressing story. Hampshire's other juniors either lived at home or went home when the season ended. For me it was not possible to return home for anything more than a visit because I had to qualify for Hampshire by residence and anyway, having made the break from my parents and from Reading, there seemed little point in returning. That doomed me to the strange, twilight world of the YMCA for some of the longest months of my life. I used to sit in my cramped and suffocating little room dreaming of the golden days of summer as the rain beat unceasingly against the windows.

I had no money to go out and it was hard to get involved in the lives of others at the hostel. After all, they were in many cases only passing through or were older and uninterested in talking to me, a seventeen-year old black boy.

Believe me, it is not easy as a young boy of the 'wrong' colour to make friends in a place like that, hard as I tried. There was little else to do on those cold, dark nights except play snooker and table football with whoever had nothing better to do. Saturday was the highlight of my tedious existence, the day I played soccer for the YMCA's A team. Sometimes I was the goalkeeper which, with my catching ability, was not the wisest position or, more often, as a winger. Covered in mud I may have been, but it was enjoyable and it kept me fit.

By now I had found myself a job at Dimplex at Southampton. With my unskilled background I had to take whatever was going. My task at Dimplex was to label and pack radiators before putting them on to trolleys. It may not have sounded much fun but I enjoyed the work and I knew it would not be anything other than temporary. If the work became boring my mind would drift back to cricket and the exciting new way of life I was forging for myself. I found my workmates to be quite congenial, in contrast to some of the inmates of the YMCA, where once again I ran into racial prejudice at its crudest. I cannot say the more permanent residents of the YMCA gave me any trouble but there were those just passing through who were ready to hurl expletives at me, usually if they considered I was spending more than my fair share of time on games like the table football. By now I had learned to ignore this kind of bigotry, however tempting it was to ram their words back down their throats. My experiences at school had taught me that it was just not worth getting into fights and, although I was not prepared to turn the other cheek, I was content to bite my lip and walk away from trouble. I was growing up.

There was a time, though, when my patience finally snapped. At long last the winter had ended and I returned to the County ground ready for my second full season as a young and ambitious county cricketer. Several of us youngsters were whitening the creases on a wicket being prepared for a county match the next day. Richard Lewis was the ring-leader when the others grabbed me and tried to smear me with the whitewash. They were just about to whiten my private parts when I broke free and, in a fit of anger, grabbed a spade. I threatened them that if they came any closer I would break it across their heads. They must have sensed this was no idle threat and they backed off hastily. Never again did I become the butt of racial jokes or of misguided horse-play at Hampshire.

It was the start of an unhappy season. More to the point, it was almost my last. Through faults, partly my own and partly the club's I came desperately close to being discarded when my contract ended in 1969. I admit my fielding was lamentable and my impetuous style of batting frequently got me out far too early to be of any real value to the team but, looking back, I remember how little help I received. How I would have loved someone to confide in. Holder was the nearest to a friend but he was newly married and had his own life to lead. The Antiguan Danny Livingstone would speak to me when the first team were around but I would have loved to have found someone with whom to share my problems, both on and off the field. None of the senior players took the trouble to sort out my weaknesses as a player, perhaps because they felt it was not their job. Remembering my own, now distant, plight I make it my business to help some of the promising young players on the Hampshire staff with the occasional word of advice —lads like Paul Terry, who has the ability to be an exceptional player, and David Rock.

Hampshire's secretary Desmond Eagar sometimes listened sympathetically to my problems but, in most cases, I had to work out my own solutions, which, as an eighteen year old miles from anything familiar, was no easy task. The statistics of 1969 show how lucky I was to be retained. Of the twelve second-team fixtures, I played in only seven of them, so providing ammunition for my biggest cause of complaint: namely, that I was being held back. I managed just 262 runs at an average of 21 with one half century, but I was never sure of my place. Most of the time I was confined to the Colts team, where I was altogether more successful, but which was not really very useful to my development. It was so easy as 420 runs from 9 innings will testify and yet, whan a vacancy arose in the second team, I was only occasionally called upon to fill it. My county colleague, Nick Pocock, was a member of the same Colts team and we had little trouble in accounting for such teams as Forest Wagtails and Portsdown Cricket Club. However, one innings which did give me pleasure was the 102 I scored against Berkshire Bantams, the team which had provided such an important part of my background.

Considering I had played in most of the second-eleven matches the previous summer, I began to feel that I was not only not making progress, I was actually going backwards. It was then that I seriously thought, for the first but not last time, of getting out of cricket. I was getting bored with picking up pieces of paper from under seats and my chances of playing against good competition were becoming rarer. Leo Harrison and I began to clash more frequently and in one heated argument I gave him a piece of my mind. It seemed to me at the time that whenever there was a vacancy in the second team it was filled by students from Southampton University including his son Martin. Sometimes there were up to four or five of them pressed into action while I, a staff man, was left to linger in the Colts.

Leo, quite rightly, pointed out how bad my fielding was and how my reckless batting was sometimes a burden to be endured by the rest of the side. He tried to get me to change my approach to batting by playing down the line and taking fewer chances. I may have been foolhardy, but I considered my batting philosophy of hitting the ball hard and often to be the best approach. I was not going to change, largely because I knew it would not work. My game was, and largely still is, built on aggression. Of course I took a risk every time I attacked the ball and on some days I paid the penalty with my wicket. The Hampshire argument was that to succeed in county cricket I had to get my head down and graft; they told me there was simply no way that my methods would bear fruit at the highest domestc level. It was a terrible dilemma. I wanted to play county cricket but should I compromise and play it their way? I remember thinking I would try to be more patient, but as soon as I reached the crease I reverted to type and with a swish of the blade would attack everything in sight and range.

Eventually at the end of the summer the coaching staff and officials gathered to discuss new conttacts. I am told that at least one recommended my release. He said I would not make the grade and it needed some careful persuasion from Mr Eagar, who had once likened me to the young Frank Worrell, to ensure my retention. Arthur Holt, too, had faith in my ability, but when the meeting took place I knew my chances were only 50–50 of getting another contract. I am pleased to say the lesson was learned. On realising how close I had come to the axe, I resolved never to let them have another chance to do this to me. No longer was I going to sulk about lack of opportunity and no longer was I going to give them cause to accuse me of letting the team down. What it came down to was this: I had been retained for my raw potential, not for my achievements.

Mr Eagar made all this plain to me and told me that he wanted a more professional response from me when we returned the following spring. It was a stern warning and I realised something had to be done. I decided to embark on a fierce and lonely struggle to make myself fitter and, more important, stronger. As the first-team players and the other youngsters went their separate ways, I was condemned to spend another winter at the YMCA with the responsibility of finding a job. It makes me laugh when I hear the anti-Packer lobby telling me how to spend my winters. When I was a teenager the same sort of people did not give a damn what I did between September and April as long as I was back and ready for action when the new county season started. As it turned out, I returned to Dimplex and labelling radiators. This time, there was no passing time on snooker and table football. Instead, virtually every night after work I went down to Northam Boys' Club to work on improving my physique. I strained and lifted weights and ran, ran and ran. Nine hours every week, often in the pouring rain or with snow on the ground, I pounded the Southampton streets in the semi-dark. I played badminton and basketball and some table tennis. Gradually a new Greenidge started to take shape, bigger and much stronger. The weights made a colossal difference and a strenuous circuit of exercises slowly strengthened my knees which had always been weak. Suddenly it was no longer possible for me to buy clothes off the peg; they had to be specially made, largely because my backside became far too large.

My self-imposed task was not without its lighter side. At midnight on a particularly foul winter night, a police car pulled alongside and beckoned me to stop. I explained I was training, which struck the policeman as a strange thing to do at that time of night. After checking with his station to see if there had been any robberies, he let me continue.

In 1970 I reported back for duty with a new contract and a new body. I was bigger, stronger, more powerful and with far more stamina. All of a sudden the complexion of my life changed. Gone too was the woolly indifference which marred my approach to cricket and fielding in particular. For hours I practised my fielding in a desperate bid to eliminate the tag of the county's worst fielder from my name. It worked, and within a matter of days the new Greenidge was apparent to everyone. Friends did not recognise the improved me nor my attitude. The coaches were shocked and pleased by the metamorphosis: their stern rebukes had obviously worked. Within days rather than weeks I was reaping the rewards of my winter's self-sacrifice and stubborn diligence. I went straight into the second team on merit. In 15 matches I scored 841 runs at an average of 32, although for the third year in succession without scoring a century. I came close to it against Glamorgan's second team at Bournemouth when I made 96 but that aside, I was a revelation. Before the season was out I had forced my way into the county side and I never looked back. The Hampshire handbook records my breakthrough.

The success of the season was 19 year old Gordon Greenidge who, after scoring consistently well for the 2nd XI, was given his chance in the county side in the closing stages of the season. So well did he accept the challenge that he made four scores of over 50 and averaged 35 runs per innings in his seven matches. His fielding improved out of all recognition and he should challenge strongly for a place in the county side for 1971.

After a season in which at last I was beginning to put my game together, the call to the first team came in strange, anti-climactic circumstances. On the morning of the match against Sussex at Bournemouth I was told to report to the ground because there was a severe injury crisis. It was only when I reached Dean Park at Bournemouth that I realised just how severe. Barry Richards, Barry Reed, Richard Gilliat, Danny Livingstone, Butch White and Bob Cottam were all ruled out and only three capped players were fit enough to take on an attack which featured England's John Snow, then at the height of his career, and Tony Greig. Roy Marshall, our captain, told me almost in passing that I was playing. In a hastily arranged batting order, I was down to go in at number six. We had lost 4 wickets for 73 when I made my way from the pavilion down the steps and out on to the pitch. I was not nervous, even at the prospect of facing Snow, just filled with a desire to make the best of my unexpected chance. Marshall was at the other end when I went in and had moved imperiously to 44 without the slightest problem while wickets had fallen at regular intervals around him. One run later he was out, and we were in trouble. The left-arm, medium-paced bowling of Mike Buss was causing the main concern. I sparred at him more than once in the early stages of my innings and then he tried to discover how I would react to a bouncer. This was what I had been waiting for. It took them 5 minutes to find the ball after I had lifted it over the ropes at backward square-leg for my first six in county cricket, the first of many. Needless to say, Buss was not a happy man. However, my one piece of belligerence was our only respite and we were all out for 150 with Buss finishing with 7 for 58. I came out of it quite well, making 24, the highest scorer after Marshall and confirming that county cricket was not so difficult after all.

Sussex went on to score 258 for 9 declared and it was up to us to save the match. This we managed without much of a contribution from me. Peter Sainsbury, as usual relishing a fight, scored 55, Lewis made 74, Jesty 73 not out and Bob Stephenson 82. Me? I made 18 before John Snow bowled me with a delivery quicker than anything I had ever encountered in junior cricket. Perhaps county cricket was not so easy. Somehow I retained my place for the next match, against Gloucestershire at Cheltenham, although I was asked this time to bat at number seven. John Mortimore's spin removed me in the first innings for 21 and Mike Procter did the damage in the second innings after I had scored three. Luckily Barry Richards, back from injury, made 94 and we won by 4 wickets with nearly an hour to spare. Richards dropped out of the following match against Glamorgan at Portsmouth and I was promoted to open with Sainsbury. Peter told me to take it gently as we walked from the pavilion to bat on that first morning, but on the third ball of the morning he was out. The setback did not worry me, and David Turner and I set about building the basis for a huge total of 412 on an easy-paced wicket. Everything went well and I had little difficulty in reaching 65 with 11 fours, before I was out. That was the breakthrough and I was in the team for the rest of the season.

Eventually on 22 August 1970, Barry Richards and I came together for the first time as Hampshire's opening pair, the start of what has been hailed subsequently as the finest opening partnership in post-war cricket. The occasion could not have been more ironic from my point of view: against Warwickshire at Edgbaston.

Nor could it have been more profitable. I scored 51 and 62 not out against an attack which included England's David Brown and the West Indian spinner Lance Gibbs. We won by 9 wickets with

Richards and I putting on 88 in the second innings. Against Leicestershire at Southampton, Barry and I did even better. Ray Illingworth, the England captain and Australian fast bowler Graham McKenzie caused us no trouble and we made 201 before Illingworth had me caught for 73. I could hardly believe my success and it was particularly gratifying to do so well at Southampton, scene of so many of my worst moments in the previous three years. It was especially pleasing to know that I did not have to pick up the waste paper next day from under those open-air stands. In all, I finished with four half centuries that summer in first-class cricket and with an average of 35 could look back with a certain amount of satisfaction. I even bowled my first ever over in county cricket against Somerset. I'm pleased to say it was a maiden but Somerset went on to win in the last over.

Events had happened quickly in 1970. I began it as a junior of such an uncertain future that I was not even sure of a place in the second team. Thanks to my winters hard graft and a dramatic change in attitude, I ended it firmly entrenched in the senior side and ready to embark on what I had every reason to suppose was going to be an exciting county career. What's more, the partnership with Richards was already beginning to take shape: another reason to view the future with genuine optimism.

3 Partnership with Richards

From the tender beginnings of my career as a county cricketer, one man was to become a vital influence: Barry Richards. Our names are now irrevocably linked, the individuals of a famous partnership. Some people will have me believe that our partnership was the best opening pairing ever to come together in one county team. I do not know about that. I am not sufficiently a student of the game to make valid comparisons. There is no doubt other counties came to fear us, but the facts appear to indicate that we were not as successful a pairing as we ought to have been. Many myths grew up about the Richards–Greenidge partnership and now I feel I should tell the truth, or at least my version of it. Did I like him? Did I hate him? Were we rivals? These are questions I am occasionally asked and now I shall put the record straight.

Barry and I could not have come from more differing backgrounds. When we first strode to the wicket together as Hampshire's opening partnership in 1970, I was a nineteen-year-old black boy from Barbados and Reading and Barry was by then the established star. Naturally, as a groundstaff boy, he was the sort of player I wished to become, but there was no way I could ever play the game the same way. Barry, a tall fair-haired man, was 25 at the time and at the height of a career which would have found its true outlet in Test cricket had he come from anywhere other than apartheid-dominated South Africa. I neither despised him for being a white South African in a land where blacks are fiercely subjugated nor did I feel sorry for him for not being able to play in any more than four Tests. To me, he was a Hampshire cricketer who, largely through his efforts in county cricket, was earning a rightful reputation as the world's best batsman.

When I first came into the team, there was a lot of ill-feeling generated by senior players, hard-bitten and past their best, against the captain, Roy Marshall. Roy had been an outstanding player in his time, a batsman of supreme ability. Now he was near to retirement and his captaincy had come in for some criticism both among the county supporters and in the dressing room, where the atmosphere was occasionally strained. Barry was the new star and there was some resentment. Not having been in the team long, I can only assume there was some jealousy, especially as Barry may have given the impression he was playing for himself. Let me say immediately that Barry was a strong individual personality who was never frightened to voice his feelings, but equally he was very much a team man. As vehemently as any other member of the Hampshire set-up, he wanted the team to be successful. No more, and no less.

Barry was, of course, a totally different batsman from me. He was a perfectionist; his timing was superb; and arrogantly, he displayed every shot in the textbook and few more besides. So much has been written about his skill, his technique and his ability to destroy any attack in the world at whim. My methods are in complete contrast. I realised from the outset there was no point in trying to be like him. My philosophy has always been to try and bury the ball into the wall of some distant building and the only way to do that is to hit it as hard as possible and as often as possible. I admired Barry for his methods and he came to admire me for mine.

In those emergency days of 1970 when so many injuries gave me my early chance in the first team, I very quickly got over my nerves and began to relish the county game. As such, I can remember no sensation of nerves when stepping out with Barry in those first few innings together. Indeed my first recollection is of him trying to suppress his laughter at my naive thrashing. Unlike other county debutants who trembled and grafted their way to a few runs, I felt the best way to make them was to attack, and this I did frequently, with occasionally disastrous consequences. Even against international bowlers I used to attack every ball. The bowlers could not believe it and I don't think Barry could either. Sometimes, after a violent swish had ended with me on my backside, I used to look to the other end to see Barry almost rocking with laughter while stunned bowlers, not used to this sort of treatment, would stare in amazement. At the end of an over he would come down and tell me to take it easy; not to be so impetuous. Not for the first time I heard the advice: 'Wait for the bad ball.' As far as I was concerned in those days of inexperienced youth, every ball—no matter who bowled it—was potentially a bad ball.

On the positive side, as an established number one with three or four years at the top behind him, he would give me some much-needed advice on how to deal with opposition bowlers. He told me what sort of delivery each was liable to test me with, which delivery to leave alone and which to attack. My first impressions of him indicated that he was not just an instinctive genius but also a thorough professional who had done his homework to an extent that he knew all their strengths and, as his record would subscribe, all their weaknesses as well.

The information he passed on was more than useful at a time when the gap between second-eleven cricket and county cricket, where I was confronted by bowlers of international standard, was so wide. I had no idea so much could be done with a ball. Some of these players, all in the space of one over, could do everything except make it talk. They would move one into me, one away from me, one up to me and one nastily short of a length. I groped and swayed to counter them as best as I could but, quite honestly, there were many times when I was absolutely baffled.

This leads me to my one major criticism of Richards as my opening partner in those first few years. As the major partner and a man revelling in the tag of the world's number one bat, he never took the responsibility of shielding me from the really top bowlers. Perhaps he felt I could and should cope on my own, yet how I would have appreciated it had he come down the wicket and said:

'You leave so and so to me.' As our leading batsman, I felt he should have helped me get over the traumas of bridging the enormous gulf between the grades. Barry once paid tribute to Robin Jackman of Surrey who, over the years, consistently claimed his wicket. What he omitted to say was that there were several other bowlers who equally often had him out and whom he secretly hated facing. John Snow of Sussex and England was one of them. Mike Hendrick, the most respected bowler on the county circuit, and his countryman, Mike Procter at his belligerent fastest, were two more against whom he was never happy. What's more, he was scared of showing it.

I think what plagued Barry more than anything was the knowledge of his own ability. He was being called the greatest contemporary batsman, but he played only in four Tests (supremely successfully) through no fault of his own, and since he was building his reputation on the fodder supplied by county bowlers, he was never sure just exactly how good he really was. That's why he always applied himself to getting runs against touring sides when they came to Southampton. And, if you look at his record, you will see a measure of his ability is that he always succeeded.

However, getting back to those first faltering steps of mine, it used to annoy me that he would not take the major bowling away from me. Sometimes against a really good bowler, early in the morning when the ball would move around, I would play and miss at four out of six deliveries. I looked a right idiot. I had no idea what to do and the flurry of raised arms from the fielders and exasperated grunts from the bowler only made my discomfiture worse. Of course, Barry had to face Procter, Snow and the other front-line bowlers and occasionally he scored runs off them, but he faced only what he considered to be his share of the attack—never more. Obviously it was quite different when we came up against moderate attacks. In that case Barry, if he was in the mood, would simply slaughter them and I was left with little to do except stand back and admire. There was a tendency occasionally for me to try to catch up when, at last, I got a chance to face the bowling and in an endeavour to do so I was often out taking a needless risk.

You may be able to understand my feelings of inadequacy when I say it was not uncommon for me to be still in single figures when the applause was ringing round the ground for his 50.

Even in later years of our partnership Richards would still avoid the top men whenever he could. I am not saying he was in any way a coward because no bowler escaped his punishment for long and, to my knowledge, he lived in deep fear of no one. But, nevertheless, I soon learned from close proximity the men who caused him anxiety and I was surprised he did not admit to more than Jackman. His failure to shield and protect me from the best county cricket could provide may, ironically, have helped my advance, although I did not see it that way at the time.

Individually, I was making progress all the time and Barry was still a fantastic batsman by any standards. We dominated the Hampshrie averages and I think it fair to say that we were major influences in the county's winning the championship in 1973 and the John Player League in 1975 and 1978, although Barry only played part of that final success. I think we were the players other counties felt obliged to remove and we made it easier for later batsmen to score freely. Both Barry and I had great days individually but, looking at the records, not as often as we should have done in tandem. The facts speak for themselves. In ten years as an established opening partnership, we exceeded 100 together on only 24 occasions. That may come as a surprise to those who considered us an outstanding pairing. And in one-day cricket we only produced century partnerships eleven times. This may account, partially, for the fact that although Hampshire twice won the JPL in our time together, we never got further than the semi-final in either of the two major cup competitions, the Gillette and the Benson and Hedges.

It may seem strange also that in ten years of trying we never did beat the county first-wicket batting record of 249 held since 1960 by Roy Marshall and Jimmy Gray. We came desperately close to it once against Kent at Southampton in 1973 in the last match of the season, just after we had clinched the championship. Barry and I scored runs at will that day against the full array of Kent bowling and there seemed nothing to stop us sailing past the record held by Marshall and Gray. Unfortunately, when we had reached 241 Barry was injured and had to leave the field. David Turner came in and we went on to amass 334 before a wicket fell. Some statisticians say that between the three of us, we broke the record; others say it should be allowed to stand because three players—and not two— were involved. Records do not bother me, but the point is, in ten years of competition, we never did overhaul a fairly modest target. Indeed, only five times in first-class cricket did we get beyond 200, starting with that 201 against Illingworth and McKenzie in my first season and continuing in the first match of the next with 233, albeit against Oxford University. During that match I scored my first century and it took us only just over three hours to get 'that many runs. Why did we never get more runs together? Probably because both of us attacked at every available opportunity and were therefore taking risks. Had we been grafters, or had one of us been a grafter, I dare say the record books would be bulging with Richards–Greenidge achievements. The truth is we had a go; sometimes we departed without having made an impression; on other occasions we took apart attacks laced with outstanding bowlers and it was by so doing that we earned our reputation as the most devastating opening partnership in county cricket during the 1970s.

In one-day cricket Glamorgan once came in for some fearful hammer from us in a Gillette Cup match at Southampton in 1975. Malcolm Nash, the Glamorgan left-arm seamer, is one of more underrated players on the county circuit and over the years he had his fair share of success against both Barry and I, especially when the conditions suit his ability to move the ball considerably. But on this day at Southampton, there was simply nothing he or his colleagues could do to halt us. There was nothing in the wicket to help him or his partners and it became one of those days where we attacked every ball . . . and it paid off handsomely. The match was played in midweek and there was by no means a big crowd to watch this calculated butchery. Barry and I put on 210 in no time, before he was out for 129 of his most brilliant runs. His departure made no difference to me and I just carried on thumping every ball bowled to me. I think Barry got himself out because he had had enough but I was enjoying it so much I decided to continue. I was named man of the match after reaching 177, a Gillette Cup record. I hit 7 sixes and 17 fours in that innings and poor old Nashy watched one six of mine sail out of the ground before producing a white handkerchief in mock surrender. Apparently the Glamorgan skipper, the Pakistani Majid Khan kept muttering on a murderously hot day: 'Oh dear . . . now what do I do?' Needless to say, Hampshire won and for those who witnessed it, the 210 put on by myself and Barry is still the partnership most talked about.

There was another glorious occasion which comes to mind. We were playing Nottinghamshire at Southampton in the 1977 Gillette Cup. Nottinghamshire had set us a by no means easy target of 216 and both Barry and I were carrying injuries which it made it difficult for us to run.

Clive Rice, the South African all-rounder and Barry Stead made us graft for our runs and it must have been as painful for the crowd as it was for us as we hobbled singles, running only when it was absolutely necessary. Barry and I decided to get the runs in boundaries if it was at all possible. Nottinghamshire tried everything they knew to break our partnership but gradually we got on top and their morale very quickly began to sink. I was first to reach 50 and Barry soon followed. My ankle injury and some problems with my knee made running an unpleasant process and with Barry also limping, we were forced to reject the chance of what would normally have been easy singles and safe twos. As Nottinghamshire wilted we both inched our way towards individual centuries. It's been suggested since that we planned it so that we each reached our centuries before the winning runs were scored. This is not true. Of course we were aware of the scoreboard and soon after I passed 100, Barry followed suit, to the delight of a large and audibly happy crowd. I won the match by despatching a six when we needed only a single. It seemed a good way to finish and anyway, neither of us wanted to run more singles. Since we

Middlesex wicket-keeper John Murray follows the progress of the ball as I sweep it to the boundary

You win some and you lose some . . . I make my lonely way back to the pavilion after a dismissal playing for Hampshire (*Southern Newspapers Ltd*)

Another boundary coming up. A cover drive on behalf of Hampshire in a
county match

Barry Richards and I relax in the slips. For many years we formed as
successful a slip-fielding partnership as a batting one for Hampshire

had each made centuries, the match adjudicator Gordon Ross had the difficult job of deciding whom should get the award. How should he choose? I had scored 13 fours and 2 sixes; Barry's runs had included 15 fours and 1 six. After much deliberation, he plumped for me because he said I had limped the most convincingly. Maybe they should have given me an Oscar instead. Nevertheless it showed how much our partnership had progressed and how by 1977 I was his equal—on his own admission.

By the start of the 1977 season, his benefit, Barry was visibly becoming bored with what he described as the endless 'chore' of county cricket. Denied the opportunity of playing Test cricket, the only outlets for his huge talent were county cricket and either Currie Cup cricket in South Africa or whatever he could negotiate for himself in Australia. It was then that he approached me and said that since I was by now playing regular Test cricket for the West Indies, I was to be the number one. From now on it was to be C. G. Greenidge and B. A. Richards, not as it had been for eight years, the other way round. It followed, in particular, my incredibly successful tour of England for the West Indies during the previous summer. I had no objections; far from it. I was flattered to think that after eight years in cricket I had overhauled a man considered by so many respectable judges, the world's best player. Having said that, in no way did I then rate myself as his successor. I had had too many falls to know that this was not true. All this was before Packer came on to the scene and gave Barry a breathtaking new outlet for his ageing talent at a time when he despaired of ever making proper use of it. It gave him a belated chance to play against Lillee and company at their peak in a situation as real as a Test match. After years of sterile mediocrity, Packer at last provided a world setting for his magnificent talent. For that, I know he will always be eternally grateful. Indeed, as I will reveal later, it was Richards who recruited me for Packer's much-maligned World Series Cricket.

While the pairing of Barry and myself had many admirers around the country and in cricket in general, there were those who detracted from Hampshire's achievement of producing such a partnership by saying that we were both expensively imported overseas stars. Certainly Barry had been brought in back in 1968 but he was then very much a novice. Although I am now referred to as an 'overseas star', I am as much an English player as any other raised and nurtured on English wickets—as much as any of my colleagues in the Hampshire team who were brought on to the groundstaff as juniors. We both have something to thank Hampshire for even if our partnership did spring forth by luck as much as judgement.

Barry once said how much he envied my ability to hit sixes consistently more often than any other player currently in county cricket. He said he just did not have similar power to attempt what for me was second nature. For him, it was completely against the grain to hit the ball in the air; every shot of which he had control, went along the ground. I do not know why he believed he did not have the power because the strength with which he struck the ball through the covers or through mid-off and mid-on, was awesome. The only time he ever hit the ball in the air deliberately was to clear in-fielders. It was cold, positive and calculated. To me, hitting sixes is the easiest thing in the world; I would not know how to hit the ball any other way and I have always felt that if other people put their mind to it, they, too, could hit more sixes. You do not have to be massively strong . . . and it's a quick way to make runs.

Of course, our time together at the wicket was not without its lighter side. There's a block of flats overlooking the ground at Southampton. The roof is not high and it's used by some nubile young ladies for sun-bathing purposes. Sometimes, in an effort to get a nice, even tan, they take off rather more than they ought . . . without realising that from the cricket ground everything is visible. Many times Barry and I have come together for what looks like a serious mid-wicket tactics discussion just to keep each other posted on what was happening up on the roof. Then on other grounds' there would be girls posturing on the boundary's edge in such a way as to draw instant attention to themselves. That, too, led to a lot of mid-wicket discussion. In the heat of the battle, it would not be uncommon for us to make social arrangements or to discuss anything but cricket. It's easy for the mind to wander even in a county match and sometimes little diversions can provide a welcome break in the gruelling concentration.

Not even cricket's lighter moments could save Barry sinking into disillusionment. His benefit season, though financially successful, demanded his attention in such a way that he found it difficult to concentrate fully on his game. Injuries did not help and at the end of the 1977 season he had failed to score 1,000 first-class runs for the first time since he joined Hampshire. The season with Packer in the winter of 1977–8 broadened his horizons and pitted him against the world's best bowlers for the first time on a truly competitive basis. When he came back in 1978 it was clear his resolve to continue with the county had gone and after a desperate bid to recapture his enthusiasm, he gave way to the inevitable. I am told there were tears in his eyes when he dictated his resignation note in the little office at the county ground. It was the end of an era and new responsibility was thrust upon my shoulders.

I can sympathise with his attitude to a certain extent. It is not difficult for me to understand what he felt about county cricket. Sometimes it can be so utterly boring as to render the game meaningless and the thought occasionally crosses my mind that I would be better employed doing something different. Towards the end of his time at Hampshire, Barry would wander down the wicket between overs and say: 'I have had enough of this.' Minutes later he was on his way back to the pavilion, the opposition celebrating but little knowing that he had given his wicket away in sheer boredom. While I sympathise with him, I love cricket too much to ever give my wicket away as he did. And when it comes the time for me to retire, it will be through old age not disillusionment. I know the alternatives and humping sacks of fertiliser is not my idea of good fun. In contrast to Barry, it will be a sad day when I leave a county ground for the last time.

Looking back on my time with Richards as a partner, I realise I was lucky. I enjoyed playing with him and I hope he enjoyed my company at the wicket. Was there a rivalry? I am not sure that I was ever conscious of it; I saw him as an example not to be copied

37

but to be emulated. It was a measure of my success when he conceded the prestigious number one spot in the Hampshire batting line-up. I'm sure, also, that he was aware of my desire for recognition. I did not wish to live continually in his illustrious shadow. Eventually as our partnership drew to a close I was out-scoring Barry and I have to admit that gave some satisfaction.

In choosing my world best team at the end of my book, you will notice I have left Barry out. This is not out of spite in any way. I have the greatest respect for him as a player and I came very close to putting him in. It so happens that I consider India's Sunil Gavaskar as the best opening batsman in the world; his record proves it. Geoff Boycott ranks among the finest but I would partner Gavaskar with someone more aggressive and, after some thought, I am forced to choose Roy Fredericks of the West Indies as his opening partner. My choice is not influenced out of any loyalty to Fredericks, I can assure you. It's just that I felt Gavaskar and Fredericks were the best-balanced opening pair I had played with or against. Had Gavasker not been chosen, then Barry might have sneaked in. Those three, and Ian Redpath of Australia, are my favourite openers; all have great personal qualities as well as batting qualities and, in my opinion, there is no one else in the contemporary game as good as that quartet.

The experience of playing alongside Barry Richards was something I shall never forget. It was an education and an inspiration. If, at the end of my career, people talk of Richards and Greenidge in the same breath, then I for one will not mind in the least.

4 First-Class Breakthrough

My success of the previous summer had still not convinced me that I should be starting the 1971 season in the first team. After all, I had only made my debut because of a long injury list and my form in those last seven matches, though promising, was by no means consistent. Barry Richards was naturally occupying one of the positions as opening batsman and I thought there were at least two ahead of me in the queue for the job of partnering him. Barry Reed, though a late entrant to county cricket, had firmly established himself as Barry's partner and Richard Lewis had shown enough glimpses of genuine talent to warrant the position of first reserve. So when we reported for training in April of that year, I was expecting a return to the second team and the prospect of waiting for further opportunities either through more injuries or through loss of form among the established men. It came, therefore, as something of a shock when I was told I would be starting as Richards's opening partner for the match at Oxford against the University. This was a tremendous opportunity to stake a claim for a regular place, and thankfully I grabbed it with two grateful hands. After bowling the University out for 200, Barry and I took their bowlers apart. We put on 233 for the first wicket, just 16 short of the Hampshire record. Barry scarcely broke into a sweat, using the bowling as valuable practice for the hard season ahead while making 133, I have to admit that I found it just as easy and rattled up 102 in 198 minutes with a couple of sixes into the bargain. I was elated by my success and suddenly realised I had played myself into the team over the heads of both Reed and Lewis.

This was confirmed when I was selected for the first county match against Northamptonshire at Southampton, and from then on I was firmly entrenched as Barry's opening partner. So entrenched that I played in 24 of our 26 matches in 1971 and passed the magic figure of 1,000 runs without as much bother as I had anticipated. It goes without saying that becoming a Hampshire regular pleased me but I cannot remember enjoying my first full season. To be candid, there were times when I wished I was back in the relative peace of second-eleven cricket, and the reasons for that had nothing to do with the game itself. Certainly I could look back on 1971 with a sense of achievement. After all I had successfully negotiated two important landmarks in the life of a county player: I had scored my first century and reached 1,000 runs. Not many people could have asked for more, so why didn't I enjoy my achievements to the full? The reasons for that lay in the terrible atmosphere of the Hampshire dressing room. Having been thrown in at the deep end it was as much as I could do to establish myself in the knowledge that county bowlers, aware of my reputation from the tail-end of the previous summer, would be keen to expose my lack of experience. If I expected any guidance from my senior colleagues, I was quickly disillusioned. Richard Gilliat, an Oxford Blue, had taken over as skipper in some controversy from the veteran Roy Marshall and the camp was deeply divided between a little clique of the more experienced men and a gaggle of youngsters all, like myself, trying to bridge huge gulf between junior and senior cricket. The older players made sure the uncapped players were aware of their status. Some of them seized upon weaknesses, traits or idiosyncrasies and mercilessly used them against us, to the extent that the dressing room became a difficult place at which to feel at ease.

The irony is that, when Marshall was captain, the more experienced men were just as avidly against him. I think it fair to say that while Roy was unquestionably one of the best batsmen of his generation as a captain he left much to be desired. The appointment of Gilliat as his replacement was hardly greeted with rounds of applause and there were many misgivings among the same players when season 1971 got under way. Gilliat, from a classic public-school background, had to prove to these hard-bitten individuals that he deserved to be skipper; that he merited their respect. With the team so inextricably divided, it was a minor miracle that we ever got together as a unit to represent Hampshire County Cricket Club. To make matters worse, there never seemed to be any logical policy to team selection. No one ever told me I would be in the team and no one gave any advice. It just appeared as if the selectors crossed their collective fingers and hoped we youngsters would pull through. But as we fought to add consistency to promise, the older players were drifting towards the end of their careers and seemingly resentful of our intrusion. One or two were determined to hold on to their places to the detriment of the team. I remember travelling to Kidderminster for a match with one (he had best remain nameless) who was patently unfit. This man, a bowler, had pulled a muscle, but rather than allow a fit replacement to travel, insisted on making the trip. He practised before the start when we all knew he was unfit and then pronounced himself ready for action. With the Worcestershire batsmen in their places and the umpires getting prepared for the match, our bowler had one final run-up practice and promptly ruled himself out, saying his injury was too bad. By then it was too late to replace him and we went through the entire match minus an important part of our attack. It was an act of pure selfishness and typical of the events of that troubled and tempestuous time.

When we did get together in the dressing room to talk cricket as a team, there were soon problems. Discussions turned into arguments and individuals, usually the youngsters, were heavily criticised. At least fears and antagonisms came out into the open on such occasions but mostly the comments were made behind backs and team morale was alarmingly low for most of my first full season. Our division was all the more plain to see on away trips where the older players stuck together, apparently refusing to mix with us. John Holder, Turner, Jesty and myself were left to form our own little group, since we were never asked to go with them to restaurants, pubs or wherever it was they went. My century against

Oxford University raised scarcely a murmur among the other players, although it meant so much to me. Nevertheless I could not escape the traditional round of drinks for first-time century-makers which it was incumbent upon me to buy. I only wish I had felt the others were genuinely sharing my achievement.

The dressing-room atmosphere aside, I made rapid developments that season as a batsman, although my impetuosity and inexperience prevented me from doing much better. Maybe after the early century against Oxford I expected to get many more. Unfortunately, every county side had at least one top-line bowler and the effort in the Parks proved to be my only three-figure success of the season. I was learning the hard way by failing to capitalise on encouraging starts and getting out to strokes which did me little credit. I learned the hard way, too, about just how hard a cricket ball can be when it's hurled at you at nearly 100 miles an hour. We were playing Essex at Westcliff when a ball from my fellow Barbadian, Keith Boyce, hit me on the head with a delivery which rose higher than I expected. I saw stars for a few moments but batted on to make 23 and although I have had my share of injuries since, my confidence has remained unimpaired.

Most players get struck at some time or another and many never fully recover their nerve. Luckily the Boyce incident did not deter me from playing my natural game and it was something of a coincidence that Boyce should inflict the injury. He was one of my earliest heroes when he played for a club near to my home in Barbados.

The end of the 1971 season saw me still without a championship century but with a thousand runs under my belt. I resolved to set myself two important targets for the following summer: a championship century and 1,500 runs. Indeed every time I reach a personal milestone, I aim for the next, and I felt that if I could achieve them both in 1972 I would be some way towards becoming a major county batsman which a couple of years earlier had been way beyond my wildest dreams. The first summer also provided me with an unexpected bonus. We were playing Surrey at Southampton at the end of the season. Surrey had won the championship the previous day and were a little the worse for wear when I was called on to bowl. With a medium-pace style all of my own, I met with little resistance and with good batsmen virtually giving their wickets away, I ended up with 5 for 49 which, to this day, is my best bowling analysis and, since I never intend to bowl much again, is likely to remain so. Surrey duly lost the match but as far as we were concerned it was something of a hollow victory against the new champions. I have never enjoyed bowling, even when I first played the game in the rough grass at Black Bess. It's an art which has to be worked at and requires a lot of painful dedication. I think I made it fairly clear that day: I was not keen to bowl regularly and my startling figures were not much more than a fluke. Hampshire took the hint and I have hardly bowled for them since. What's more, in something like twenty Tests for the West Indies I have been asked to bowl only one over. It was at Melbourne in the Third Test in 1975–6 and although Australia were close to beating us, I'm proud to say it was a maiden.

Interesting and rewarding the summer may have been, but the winters still represented a major problem. Now that I was established in the Hampshire first team, I desperately wanted to broaden my experience by playing abroad but as September came there was no alternative but to start looking for a job locally. Some of the senior players had coaching jobs in South Africa; obviously there was a fat chance of me being able to do that, but it was with a great feeling of anti-climax that I started scanning the columns of the local papers for temporary jobs. So, as the others went their separate ways for the winter I found myself signing on for some work at Southampton Airport. My task for six purgatorial months was to underseal Ford Transit vans with the 'bonus' of a bit of stocking for delivery. Quite simply I had to do something to keep me going for the cold, dark months but the more success I was having as a cricketer, the harder it was to go back to mundane winter jobs. I hope that does not sound arrogant. What I meant to say was that having achieved the breakthrough at an important level, there seemed little point in wasting my time at a job which could have no ultimate bearing on my career as a cricketer.

Unskilled and with a limit to what I could choose, I was forced to take whatever was available. I was still living in the YMCA in a cramped little box to which I returned every boring evening after a hard day at Fords. I was desperately lonely and very unhappy. By their nature, the YMCAs are for passing through so it was difficult to make lasting friendships with people who were probably gone next day. I cannot remember ever having any close friends and certainly no girl friends. To make matters worse, I was not earning much and there was little money to spare on going out. I did not drink much and places like discos can be as lonely as sitting in your own room if, like me, you are a black boy in a white city.

My only diversions were an occasional visit to the cinema or going out with someone new from the YMCA for a night on the town, if I could afford it, and then clambering up drainpipes to get back in again. Those sorts of nights were rare and for the most part I had no alternative but to hold my own counsel in a sea of ever-changing faces and to think ahead to the summer as solace and comfort. John Holder was my one true friend. We were from the same West Indian background and with the same desire to succeed at cricket with a club with whom we had no natural allegiance through birth or length of residence. Holder had just got married and was more than busy getting together his first home, but in 1971 he had only played in seven first-team matches because of injury and there was a nagging fear in his mind that he was not going to make the grade, either through injury or lack of opportunity. It may have been his company, I am really not sure, but once again I began to have doubts that I wanted to be a full-time cricketer. Full time is something of a misnomer because it was the long, dreary winters during which I was left to fend for myself that really got me down. Hampshire, through no great fault of their own but because of the system, were not in a position to care what I did in the winter and it was this feeling of isolation which led me into thinking about a permanent career outside the game. Holder, wracked by self-doubt, thought along the same lines and we enrolled at a night-school class in Southampton to study elementary accountancy. I don't think we studied accountancy for any specific reason but my lack of educational qualification and the insecurity of a cricketer's life made me aware of the many years of my life still ahead and of one thing I was certain . . . I did not want to be undersealing Fords as a permanent way of making a living.

Holder's decision to make use of his spare time proved wise. Injury got the better of him after another truncated season and he was forced to quit, a shattering blow to any man in what should have been the prime of his career. Holder was meant to be one of our main strike bowlers for the 1972 season because Hampshire, in the throes of transition, had taken the rejuvenation process a step or two further during the winter. Butch White had not been retained, a decision which infuriated him after so many years of faithful and successful service, and he had gone off to play one-day games for Glamorgan. Alan Castell had also been forced to drop out of the game through injury and then Bob Cottam, another Test player, decided not accept another contract and joined Northamptonshire instead. This meant that apart from Holder there was no pace attack of any kind. In addition Danny Livingstone, a veteran of the 1961 championship-winning side, was sacked and given a benefit all at the same time. It was against this background that another long winter ended and I reported for the pre-season build-up once again determined to continue the progress of preceding seasons. This time I expected to start in the team, though the batting was the least of our worries. There was Richards, Marshall, Gilliat, myself, Turner and Jesty but the bowling was going to cause us problems. Bob Herman, a fast-medium swing bowler, was imported from Middlesex, though he had been born in Southampton and qualified immediately. Herman had not been successful at Middlesex and the thought of him opening our attack with Holder would hardly have sent shivers of fear down the spines of our opponents. Having spent the winter keeping fit by playing table tennis, badminton and the occasional game of soccer at Northam Boys' Club, I felt in good order when we began the 1972 season.

Herman, with so much to prove, was instantly successful and the new-look Hampshire did rather better than their supporters

45

might have imagined after the upheavals of the close-season. We finished in ninth place in the championship and sixth in the John Player League. For me there were two major objectives: to surpass my total of 1,164 runs of the previous summer and to score my first championship century. The second of my immediate ambitions was achieved at Chelmsford in only the second championship match of the season. It came a few days after we had played the Australians at Southampton and where for the first time I came across a young fast bowler by the name of Lillee. Lillee did not get me out in either innings but there was enough about him to suggest that he could become a major influence in world cricket. Now I regard him as the best bowler of his type in the world and the man I least enjoy facing, for reasons I shall reveal later.

My first century, was achieved largely against the spinners. The crafty leg-spin of Robin Hobbs almost got me out several times but I got my revenge by lifting him for a couple of sixes and the 124 I made that day was another important breakthrough. Keith Boyce was, with John Lever, their main strike bowler and the thought of scoring my maiden championship century against an attack which included him was stimulating. For me the hundred marked the end of a long struggle but I told myself that it was only the start of something better. A milestone had been reached, but rather than wallow in self-congratulations I made up my mind it was to be the first of many. I resolved to set myself a new goal—my county cap, which provides financial benefits and recognition from all concerned that you have made the grade. Little did I realise, but this particular issue was to cause me more than a little irritation.

Herman had not long been with Hampshire before he received his county cap. Now, I have no wish to belittle the achievements of 'Lofty' either that season or for what he did subsequently for Hampshire. But after a comparatively short time as the county's number one pace bowler, he was capped. Since I had by now been a regular and increasingly important part of the team, I was furious that he had been given his cap ahead of me. I made my feelings well known and eventually felt sufficiently aggrieved to confront

Gilliat about the matter. What I wanted to know was why Herman had jumped in front of me in the queue and when Hampshire would see fit to give me mine. Gilliat did his best to be diplomatic but his excuses at the time seemed poor. He said Herman had done well for us—which he had—and that he had been unlucky at Middlesex. I couldn't quarrel with what he said, but was still unable to tell why he had been rewarded before I had. I was told in a non-committal sort of way that if I continued to graft and improve, then I too would be capped.

It was with a sense of indignation that I went about my business for the remainder of the summer. My list of achievements grew almost daily but the financial limitations of not being capped were beginning to get me feeling depressed and puzzled. Sir Leonard Hutton recognised my talent by awarding me the man of the match gold medal for scoring 81 in the Gillette Cup against Minor Counties South at Southampton and I was making enough reasonable scores to deserve recognition from Hampshire. My fellow Barbadian and later one of my greatest friends, Vanburn Holder, caused me my most unpleasant moment at Portsmouth. Van has since become my room-mate when touring with the West Indies and with Barbados. But on a fast track, he got one to rise sharply and it hit me in the mouth. I needed seven stitches and a lot of dental treatment on some loose teeth as a result of this little setback, but luckily my confidence and approach were not affected any more than temporarily.

To confirm my growing ability to cope with the demands of county cricket, on a fast wicket at Hove in August I compiled my biggest score to that date against an attack which included John Snow and Tong Greig. It was achieved on a wicket helpful to players with international reputations but the main significance, as far as I was concerned, lay in the length of time it took me to score the runs. I made 142 in something like five hours. Now, to someone like me who has made his name as a fast scorer, this may seem an odd admission. Truth to tell, I was particularly pleased to have taken so long to make the runs. Never before had I been so long at the crease and it was becoming crucial to me to build a big innings, for no other reason than just to see if I could do it. I had at last begun to realise that if I was to fulfil my promise, to make the best of my ability, I had to play a long innings. I remember having a few early problems with Snow and company but gradually I settled and started, quite deliberately, to take my time and in so doing, ignore deliveries I would have normally attacked. I had no intention ultimately of changing my approach but the need for a big and long innings was becoming important at this stage of my career and I was greatly pleased to have finally accomplished it. Never before had I gone out of my way to play an innings in a certain manner just to see what it was like. The result represented an important step towards self-knowledge: I could now play any type of innings on my terms. I think it was then that I realised for the first time that I had it in me to become something above an ordinary county player, although there was much work still to be done.

As the season drew to a close, I was still anxiously awaiting news of my cap which, in my opinion, was well overdue. I had duly surpassed my run total of the previous summer and with an aggregate of 1,230 at an average of 33, I was satisfied with my progress. What surprised and irritated me was that Hampshire did not apparently share my view and the Herman affair was beginning to niggle me more and more. Eventually, just before the season ended, I was told in the dressing room as we were about to go out to play that there was a surprise for me. At the bottom of the stairs, Richard Gilliat presented me with my much-coveted cap and the worries and resentments disappeared almost immediately the cap was clasped in my hands. It may only be a piece of cloth worth next to nothing, but its significance makes it vital and valuable. It guaranteed me more money and provided the chance of a potentially lucrative benefit ten years hence. It also gave me status and recognition, both of which I craved every bit as much. I can look back on it now as a major turning point of my career. At 21 I was a senior player on merit and there was nothing I could not achieve providing I had my share of luck and providing I continued to work hard.

It was now vital for me not to waste my time in the winter and it was with some pleasure that I received an invitation from the cricket board of Barbados inviting me out for the winter to play in the Shell Shield team. It was just what I had been hoping for and a chance to visit the island I had not seen since I left to rejoin my mother some six or seven years before. The offer was simple enough. The board would pay my fare to and from England and it was up to me to get myself a job in Barbados, one which would give me plenty of time to play for the island in the fiercely competitive inter-island Shield.

As we flew from the darkening, wintry skies of England towards the Barbados sun, I was in a jaunty and optimistic mood. I had done well in England. I was securely capped and now, on a plate, was the chance to gain experience on the hard and fast West Indian wickets and to impress the West Indian Board of Control. Some of the great West Indian players such as Wes Hall, Charlie Griffith, Conrad Hunte, Seymour Nurse and Basil Butcher were either going or gone and even the great Gary Sobers was coming to the finale of an unparalleled career. In short, there were places in the West Indian team to be grabbed by any one showing temporary good form or permanent quality. Sobers was still in the West Indies team, of course, and so were Rohan Kanhai and Lance Gibbs, but the other places were not being filled as easily as they had been in the past and I was feeling as we travelled that a good campaign for Barbados in the Shield might secure me a place in the West Indian team to tour England the following summer. It was not such a naive ambition as it may sound. There was not much competition for the opening-batsmen positions and a good winter might clinch me a surprise place.

The sight of the palm trees gently bending in the wind from the plane was a welcome sight but if I thought I was returning to a hero's home-coming, I was in for a terrible shock. I thought I was going back to my people; to the people among whom I was born and nurtured; back to relatives and family friends. How wrong I was. My family were friendly enough but for the rest, I was in for a stunning let-down. For reasons I could not understand immediately I was a stranger in my own country, a victim of a strange hate campaign which both worried and unnerved me to such a degree that I seriously considered an early return to England.

Not wishing to live back in St Peter's again, I booked into—you've guessed it—the YMCA in Bridgetown. My mate Vanburn Holder and I were fixed up with jobs working in a sort of public relations capacity for the island's brewery, Banks Brewers. Our job helped us to learn all about brewing but it entailed going out and meeting the people of Barbados and it was then that my problems began. I was amazed at the hostile reaction towards me—a sort of racial prejudice in reverse. A typical reaction was: 'Hello, Englishman. What makes you so great?' Those sorts of things hurt me deeply. I could not understand why my own people were turning against me. The abuse continued and worsened whenever I played for Barbados. To help their cause I was not very success-ful. In six matches I scored only 368 runs at an average of 30 and a hail of abuse greeted me every time I was out. 'Go home, English-man. Who the hell are you?' It was only later that I realised why they resented me so much. They felt I was taking the place of home-grown players; that I was in a privileged position purely because of a couple of moderate seasons in English cricket.

I must have seemed like an outsider at the wicket. Raised on soft English wickets and against medium-paced swing bowlers, I was caught unawares by the local conditions. The bowlers were faster, the wickets were quicker and bouncier and the glare caused me many troubles. My eyes started to water in the heat and glare and the bright sunlight accounted for me as many times as the bowlers. Obviously I needed to win over the Barbadian fans with a big innings but I returned to England without a century and with the prejudice still as rampant as when I first arrived 'home'.

The lack of glare makes night cricket very attractive to me, but I am not using it as too much of an excuse. I was taken by surprise by the conditions and by the incredible reaction among the sup-porters, and I did myself less than justice. But just when my morale was at its lowest ebb, I was summoned to Montego Bay in Jamaica to play for the West Indies Board President's XI against

My county cap. With me after the presentation are Danny Livingstone (left) and fellow Barbadian Roy Marshall, a former Hampshire captain and one of their greatest post-war players (*Southern Newspapers Ltd*)

Catches win matches . . . Alan Mansell of Sussex caught Greenidge, bowled Sainsbury. Bob Stephenson is the wicket-keeper and Barry Richards stands by in case of mistakes. A scene in a county match, Hampshire v Sussex at Southampton (*Southern Newspapers Ltd*)

Viv Richards (left), playing for Somerset, watches as another shot brings four runs. Brian Close wisely stays crouching (*Southern Newspapers Ltd*)

Presentation time. Commentator Brian Johnston hands over a man of the match award

the touring Australians, a step which confirmed I was in the eyes of the selectors. There was a big crowd and since it was something of a trial match for the impending tour of England, the West Indian players took it as seriously as any Test match. I fared quite well, though I am not sure how many runs I made and returned to Barbados full of expectancy. The harassment from the fans at the Kensington Oval continued but in spite of my mediocre performances, the selectors no doubt had me on their short list for the tour. I reasoned that although I was a novice on the hard wickets of my native country, as an 'English' player I was increasingly effective in English conditions. As far as I could make out, Roy Fredericks was a certainty for one of the opener positions but the choice for the other lay between Steve Camacho, the white Barbadian Geoff Greenidge and myself. Geoff Greenidge had played one or two outstanding innings for the West Indies but was not consistent, least of all in England where his career for Sussex had not developed from promising beginnings.

The party was announced and I was not in it. I was hugely disappointed and filled with a resolve to prove the selectors wrong. I caught the plane back to England, much wiser for the winter in Barbados and determined to make 1973 a season in which Gordon Greenidge would become so important that the West Indies could no longer ignore him. And what better chance than with them touring England. Never have I been so anxious to prove to so many people that they had made a terrible mistake.

5 Road to the Championship

After the disappointments of the winter, I returned to Southampton to prepare for the new county season as I have never prepared before or since. Irritated by my rejection by the West Indies for the tour and perplexed by my mediocre season with Barbados, I trained in a manner befitting an Olympic athlete. Every day I pounded the streets, up and down The Avenue, one of Southampton's main thoroughfares, and around and around the county ground, hour after hour in the chill of the spring winds. I must have clocked up hundreds of miles a week, running alone and driven on by a desire to prove so much to so many people. In particular I wanted to prove to the West Indies they had made a mistake and to prove to Hampshire that having got my cap, I could now go on and become a batsman of international class. Talking of the Olympics, I think if I had been entered for the Marathon I would have stood a chance of a gold medal because I have never been fitter. When I was not running I was working on the weights and undergoing the hell of circuit training. Deep down I was determined to make 1973 count for something personally and so it proved to be. It was also a significant year for Hampshire because against all the odds we won the county championship for only the second time in a history spanning more than a hundred years. How we accomplished it, I'm still not entirely sure. However, our rivals would be bound to admit that we were worthy champions because we went through the season unbeaten in 20 championship matches and were 31 points clear of Surrey, the runners-up. Incredibly, the team, on paper at least, was weaker than for many years and certainly weaker than in 1972 when we managed to win only four of our games.

Roy Marshall retired after the 1972 season and John Holder, one of our main strike bowlers, was finally forced out of the game by injury. There was no obvious replacement for Marshall, who would have been difficult to replace at the best of times, and the bowling appeared frail and inexperienced. Mike Taylor, a talented all-rounder surprisingly released by Nottinghamshire, was recruited to bolster our middle order and our pace attack, which was desperately short of genuine speed and hostility. Our spin attack consisted of the wily veteran Peter Sainsbury and a young and untried New Zealander, David O'Sullivan, both of whom made important contributions to our unlikely championship success. But the man who shocked everyone—opponents and ourselves alike—was a lanky beanpole of a bowler called Tom Mottram. 'Motters' must have been 6 foot 4 inches and both slim and unathletic. He came to us in his mid-20s from Loughborough College and after a few games the previous season, suddenly found himself sharing the new-ball attack with Bob Herman. Now part of our success lay in our tremendous fielding. We caught some sensational catches and backed up our limited bowling by making it difficult for opponents to pierce the field with some equally brilliant stops. Motters, who became known as the Pink Panther, because he walked in the same way as the cartoon character, was the world's worst fielder and he could not bat either. Indeed it was something of a minor miracle if he ever scored a run, as his season's total of 51 will testify. For all that, he played a vital part in our success, taking 57 wickets at an average of 22 and regularly dismissing the best batsmen in the country. Time and again, Mottram got rid of the most important man in our opponents' batting line up, opening the way for the rest of our bowlers to inflict the severest damage.

Geoff Boycott was so often a victim of Mottram's that he virtually became his 'rabbit' and he was by no means the only player of world renown to fall victim of his deceptively ambling approach. Tom was a great and humorous character who was vital

53

to team morale and I only wish after denigrating his fielding and his bowling that I could say he was an outstanding bowler. But, as other members of the championship-winning side will also tell you, Mottram was really very ordinary. He had no pace and he seldom deviated the ball. Literally, he used to con batsmen into believing he was a better bowler than he appeared. From the side, it may have looked as if he was getting pace off the wicket with the ball coming down from his great height. This was not so. I think he got his wickets through lack of pace and through lack of deviation because time after time he would lope up to the wicket and deliver a ball that was not fast and not doing anything. Yet just as often, this gentle giant took the all-important wickets. Standing at slip, which I did most of that summer, I could see what bowlers were doing or, in Tom's case, not doing. And every time he took a wicket he had a ready-made explanation on how it was achieved, and always with his tongue in cheek. Typical of this was when we played Northamptonshire at Southampton in the middle of August with the championship race beginning to become competitive. Northants were our nearest rivals at the time and a win was important for both sides. England's obdurate David Steele, grey-haired and bespectacled, was the man we needed to remove above all others. On a wearing wicket, Steele lunged forward defensively at Tom and the ball jumped over his shoulder. Bob Stephenson took it standing 10 or 12 yards back. Steele stood transfixed outside his crease and Bob gently rolled it back along the ground to stump him by inches. We could hardly believe our luck as the bemused Steele traipsed dejectedly back to the pavilion with 2 to his name. Tom had an instant explanation: 'It was such a good ball, he felt I deserved a wicket with it.' With Steele out twice cheaply to Tom, we won inside two days by 7 wickets and the most difficult hurdle of the season was safely negotiated.

Tom never achieved any particularly remarkable performances but his contribution to the team both on and off the field was inestimable. After 1973 he played only another 14 first-class matches before disappearing from the scene as quietly as he came on it. Nowadays he is an architect, based at Poole in Dorset, and I am told he does not even play club cricket.

Before the championship season really got under way, we played against the West Indies touring side at Southampton in a match I had been looking forward to ever since the Board had made it clear I was not yet ready to be seriously considered for the Test team. Barry Richards was rested and out too were Gilliat, Mottram and Stephenson, for no other reason than to give the youngsters a chance. One of these youngsters was a young Antiguan fast bowler who had been learning his trade in the second team. Andy Roberts could not play in the first team because we had our quota of overseas players already. Andy was over-eager to impress and the West Indies beat us comfortably by 174 runs. I, too, must have been over-anxious because my scores of 9 and 13 must have confirmed in the selectors' minds that they were right to ignore me, but Andy, who finished with match figures of 1 for 144, did strike one telling blow. Steve Camacho, who opened with Roy Fredericks, was the unlucky victim. One of Andy's deliveries in the second innings struck poor Steve in the face, inflicting such a bad injury that he was unable to continue on the tour. Obviously I was sorry about what had happened to Steve but his prolonged absence forced the West Indies to start looking for a replacement, since by that time the Test series itself had not even started.

Lawrence Rowe, the Jamaican batsman who had promised to become one of cricket's great players, had not been able to tour because of ankle ligament trouble. So he was out of the running as a possible replacement. Geoff Greenidge of Sussex had had Test experience and had scored a century against Hampshire only recently. He was a likely candidate. I figured that I, too, was in the selectors' thoughts as they narrowed the choice. I had started the season well with five scores of 50 or more and my biggest score so far, 196 not out against Yorkshire at Headingly. I was the man in form and there seemed no logical alternative from elsewhere. Imagine then, how stunned I was when I heard that Ron Headley of Worcestershire had been called up by the West Indies over the heads of us all. No disrespect to Ron, but it was an amazing decision and one which left me in a state of shock for what seemed like weeks. Ron was the Jamaican-born son of the great George Headley. He had been brought up in Birmingham and had played loyally and comparatively successfully for Worcestershire for fifteen years without ever once so much putting himself in line for a cap, or without ever doing anything to suggest he had been unlucky. Yet here he was, at the advanced age of 34, hoisted from obscurity into the touring party and into contention for a Test place. Indeed he went on to play in the first two Tests at the Oval and Edgbaston, scoring 62 runs in four innings. Everything was right for me to fill the gap and I was deeply distressed when Headley jumped the queue ahead of me. I thought my chances were especially good after the innings at Headingly, a month before the Camacho incident.

The resentment over the initial rejection still with me, I was determined to make them pay for leaving me out and it was the Yorkshire bowlers who suffered. It had to be someone and it just so happened it was them. Geoff Boycott helped Yorkshire reach 168 and for the next day or so I vented my anger on their bowling, carrying my bat for 196. I hit a couple of sixes, one of which I remember clubbing so hard that it went far over the longest boundary into the stands where it was never found. They had to find a replacement before play could continue. The innings got me a few headlines and I had hoped done my future Test chances some good.

It took me a long time to get over Headley's elevation, although I had absolutely nothing against him personally. I could not understand why, apart from his experience, he had been chosen in front of me and, rather petulantly, I went away and sulked. Perhaps they thought I was too young but it got to the stage where thereafter I really did not care whether the West Indies won or lost and whenever the highlights came up on television, I switched them off. If nothing else, at least I was learning about the weird ways in which teams were selected.

When it became apparent that the West Indies thought they could do without me, England became interested in my international future. Since I had lived in England for seven years I was qualified to play by residence and the thought had crossed my mind that perhaps I should be prepared to play for England instead.

I was in a bit of a dilemma. I was keen to play for the West Indies but if they did not want me I had to find some other way of playing Test cricket. I reasoned that I had been invited to play for Barbados for a specific purpose: to let the selectors have a closer look at me in different conditions. But the rebuff had hit me hard and England must have sensed that they stood a chance of persuading me to play for them. It was at about this time that England made their approach.

Charlie Knott, the chairman of Hampshire's cricket committee, cornered me at Bournemouth and said that he had been asked by England to discover whether I would be interested in playing for them. I was surprised, a little flattered maybe, but put on the spot, I told Charlie that I was prepared to wait a little longer to see if the West Indies changed their minds. I made it clear to him that if I was still being ignored in a year or two, then I would be only too pleased to switch allegiance.

I have often wondered since then what would have happened if I had opted to play for England. At the time, the offer—such as it was—was tempting and England supporters will never know how close I came to accepting the veiled proposition.

The West Indies went on to win two of the three Tests and with Clive Lloyd the heir apparent to Sobers and Kanhai, a new and exciting team was beginning to take shape. Alvin Kallicharran was making a middle-order spot his own and Boyce and Bernard Julien were causing all sorts of problems as the strike bowlers. Kanhai and Sobers were nearing the end of their Test careers and, most important for me, there was a gap for an opener. I resolved to ignore England's call for the time being and to press myself into the West Indies team on sheer weight of runs.

Somehow I managed to subdue my resentment and began to play a significant part in Hampshire's growing title challenge. Apart from Barry Richards, we had no world-class players but each one of the thirteen players we used made a vital contribution at some stage in the season, usually just when it mattered. The greater our success, the better the team spirit became and the more difficult it became for opponents to conquer us. Many of the better-fancied counties could not believe that our hastily assembled team of rejects, overseas players and solid county professionals would last long enough to carry off domestic cricket's greatest prize. Yet as the weeks drifted by, we beat all our major rivals when it mattered and, after the heavy defeat of Northamptonshire inside two days in August, there was never any doubt in our minds that we would go on and clinch the championship. For the record, our thirteen were: B. A. Richards, C. G. Greenidge, D. R. Turner, R. M. C. Gilliat (captain), T. E. Jesty, R. V. Lewis, A. J. Murtagh, P. J. Sainsbury, M. N. S. Taylor, D. R. O'Sullivan, G. R. Stephenson (wicketkeeper), R. S. Herman, T. J. Mottram.

I played in all our matches and ended the season as our heaviest scorer by well over 300 runs. In all, I made 1,656 at an average of nearly 49. Richards played in fewer matches but averaged 51 in making 1,326 runs. A curious aspect, looking at the figures of that memorable season, was that we were the only players to score more than 1,000 and only four of us made centuries. It would seem then, that Barry and I carried the rest of the team to the title, but this was by no means the case. Everyone did something important and both the bowling and fielding were of an exceptionally high standard.

Mottram took 57 wickets in first-class matches, Sainsbury 53, Taylor 64, Jesty 36, Herman 64 and O'Sullivan 47, including 31 of them in some fantastically sustained spells of left-arm spin bowling in August, just when the pressure was at its greatest. I suppose if I have to choose a turning point in a season of great success, it was the match against Warwickshire at Coventry early in June when several teams were jostling for a position at the top of the championship table. Warwickshire were laced with international players: there was former England captain Mike Smith and three other England players in John Jameson, David Brown and Bob Willis and in Kallicharran and Deryck Murray, two current West Indian Test men. This was a formidable array of top-class players in comparison with our line-up which had Richards's limited Test experience as our only reply. But on a beautiful wicket at Coventry, we slaughtered Warwickshire with what must rank as our best display of the year. I helped Barry put on 119 for the first wicket before I was out for 56, but Barry went on unchecked to make his biggest score in English cricket. When he was finally out he had hit 38 fours and 3 sixes in making 240. Warwickshire, chasing 396, were forced to follow on by some good all-round bowling and in their second innings Mottram took 6 wickets for 63 and, to our own intense surprise, we were left only 35 to win. This we did with ease. Warwickshire were champions at the time and it was their first defeat since August 1971. The world of county cricket was shocked, not just by our victory but by the extent of it, and suddenly it dawned on us that the title was there for the taking.

The match after our defeat by the West Indies tourists, I scored 109 against Somerset but an innings which stands out in the memory was at Southport in July where we played Lancashire. Once again our bowlers made the opposition graft for 214 and then Barry and I went to work, putting on 200 for the first wicket in only 57 overs. I went on to score 153 and in so doing passed the 1,000 mark for the third successive time. Achieving the 1,000 so early in the season lifted me considerably and a new target of an additional 500 did not seem too fanciful. Trevor Jesty bowled them out quickly in the second innings and we won by an innings and 74. Next day we were at Worcester, where we built a first innings lead of 13 and, in making 302 for 4 in three hours, I made my fourth century of the season—104 against a bowling line-up of Basil D'Oliveira, Norman Gifford and Imran Khan. Our bowlers did the rest and we were home and dry by 191 runs. All of this now represents just a mass of facts, but the significance of those two wins turned the race our way after a succession of drawn matches during which it seemed our early victories might count for nothing.

By now I was taking up for the first time what has since become my favourite fielding position. My early fielding, you will remember, almost cost me dearly at Hampshire but I had improved sufficiently to be offered the chance of fielding slip when we met Glamorgan at Swansea. Barry, who had performed brilliantly there for several seasons, was injured and his absence thrust me into that most important of catching positions. The move did wonders for my concentration and I am positive that it also made me a much better batsman. For the first time in my career as a reluctant fielder I had to watch every ball, as if I was batting myself, with the knowledge that with our limited bowling it was important I held a vast proportion of the catches which came my way.

I found fielding in the slips to be good fun above all else and I became aware that if I ever failed with the bat, I could still make some kind of valuable contribution. Through sheer hard work and solid practice I can now probably throw a cricket ball a considerable distance, though I'm not sure exactly how far. One of these days I shall throw a ball for no other reason than to see how far it goes, but there are several in the West Indian team who are at least my equal in that department and some like Viv Richards and Michael Holding who may well be better. As for slip fielding, it was crucial we held our close-to-the-wicket catches in 1973 and when Barry returned he and I lined up at first and second slip, alongside wicketkeeper Bob Stephenson. I think it fair to say that the three of us helped win some important matches and there was little during the summer which escaped us, so inspired was our catching. Indeed the three of us took 130 catches, which is a disproportionately large number. Stephenson held 59 catches and I pipped Barry by one catch (36 to 35) at slip. Our success encouraged our bowlers to bowl to us behind the stumps and they responded far better than we had dared hope before the season's start. With us holding virtually everything which came our way, the bowlers had the increasing confidence to swing the ball away from the batsmen towards the slips and in match after match, the simple ploy worked like a dream. I loved every minute of it at slip and I could not help musing how much of a contrast it all was from those dark early days standing in a world of my own at fine-leg and third man, as far away from the bat as possible and then incurring the wrath of my team-mates as I let the ball trickle harmlessly through my legs for four. In a matter of four years I had developed from the worst fielder imaginable into an excellent slip catcher.

With the growing realisation that we were in with an exceptionally good chance of winning the title, August was going to prove a desperately crucial month for us. It represented five matches, all of them at one or other of our home grounds: Southampton, Bournemouth and Portsmouth. Portsmouth was where we started our run-in at that least pretty of county grounds. The wicket at this government-owned ground always used to be fast and helpful to the quicker bowlers but here the gentle left-arm spin of David O'Sullivan began to make what turned out to be the decisive contribution of our championship season. Against Essex in our first match of Portsmouth Week, it was the pacemen who were responsible for bowling them out in the first innings for 180 and when all but one other failed to reach double figures, Turner (98) and Gilliat (110) saw us to a comfortable 73 run first-innings lead. Rain intervened on the second day and we were left to interminable games of cards in the dressing room as it fell from the skies. With little prospect but to bat out time, Essex began to dig themselves in and O'Sullivan was the man chosen to winkle them out. He bowled 27 consecutive overs and took 6 for 35, to leave our opponents groping at 113 for nine, but the rain had done its damage and we ran out of time. Since the match was drawn and we had collected only 9 points it was vital we beat Derbyshire at Portsmouth in the next match. Derbyshire have never been brisk scorers in the time I have been playing county cricket and it took them a tedious 111 overs to score 176 but they did have an excuse. O'Sullivan was pinning them down with another marathon stint of sustained accuracy. In 38 overs he took 4 for 60, opening the way for Gilliat to score another century and enabling us to build a substantial first innings lead of 202. Sully then bowled another 41 overs and with Peter Sainsbury picking up wickets with his slow-left-arm spin, Derbyshire quietly crumbled and we needed only two to win. That was achieved first ball.

It goes without saying that the 21 points we picked up with the defeat of Derbyshire did us a power of good and the stage was set for the match with second-placed Northamptonshire at Southampton. The county ground was packed as never before and once again it was O'Sullivan's inspired bowling which turned the match irrevocably our way. The great Indian spin bowler Bishen Bedi prevented us getting any more than a 59 run first-innings lead by taking 6 wickets, but with the help of Mottram, Sully took 4 for 50 and, as you will recall, we won by 7 wickets with a day to spare.

My own contribution in these three matches had been by no means substantial and I have to admit I really did not do very much in the comprehensive demolition of Nottinghamshire at the start of Bournemouth Week. Bournemouth was the scene of the county's last major honour in 1961 and it was to Dean Park that we came towards the end of a hectic and traumatic month, our nerves beginning to fray as the enormity of our impending achievement became more apparent. My first innings score of 30 did only a little to help us reach 263 but, as so often in 1973, all but one player reached double figures. Then O'Sullivan continued his golden month by taking a career-best 6 for 26 and leaving us with a lead of 136. I failed again in the second innings with a personal score of 12 but others, especially Gilliat, got the runs when we most needed them and we left Nottinghamshire a day to get 345. In less than two hours of the third day it was all over. Nottinghamshire were all out for 49 with O'Sullivan ripping through them and ending with 5 for 15. He received a standing ovation on the way back to the little pavilion; his match figures of 11 for 41 had put the championship tantalisingly near our grasp.

We went into our final match, against Gloucestershire at Bournemouth, needing only a few points to clinch the title and in no mood to let it all slip away from us. Mike Taylor took 7 wickets in the Gloucestershire innings and at last I played a crucial part in the championship coming to Hampshire by making 96 in our total of 307, a lead of 103. At 4pm on the second day, we became champions when we reached our fifth batting point. O'Sullivan took three more wickets in the second Gloucestershire innings and with a quick 65 I helped us win by 5 wickets. Needless to say, the celebrations continued for what seemed like days, normally sober players behaving as never before and enough champagne being consumed to launch a ship. The more I think about it, the more incredible it all seems. We had few stars, hardly a class player and yet everyone did his bit. If anyone failed there were no recriminations and no criticism in the dressing room. It was a pleasure to play in such a happy atmosphere and for this Richard Gilliat must take some of the credit. Within two years of inheriting a deeply divided and ageing team, he had been instrumental in raising morale from the floor and turning a motley group of individuals into champions. In 1973 his greatest asset was to get the best out of ordinary players and to do the obvious at the right time. I have never thought of him as a particularly brilliant tactician but he made few mistakes with the limited resources at his disposal, and for that he won our unwavering respect. I think he was at his best during the last, so important month when, with other teams breathing down our necks, the pressure became intense and fierce. We could so easily have blown everything by simply not having the nerve to cope. Similar things have happened to teams both before and since and will doubtless happen again. Nerve and will to win were as vital assets in August as anything else, and it was Gilliat who instilled in us the need to keep going and to disregard the pressure.

He insisted on pre-match conferences during which we discussed the opposition, the wicket, our tactics and where he made it clear that he expected us not to wilt in the face of the ever-increasing necessity to keep winning. The national press were beginning to follow us around as the championship neared its end and it was hard to pick up a paper in August without us figuring prominently on the sports pages. Gilliat told us not to let this increase the pressure and with coolness and deliberation he handled all radio and television interviews without revealing anything of the worry he and the rest of us were feeling. At times we found it difficult to keep the momentum. It only need a few showers to send morale crashing and defeatist talk started to creep into our vocabulary. The skipper would have none of this even if he was feeling exactly the same himself, and there were times when little personal lectures pulled us up sharp and had us all thinking positively again. It's

63

fair to say Gilliat forced us over those final hurdles by his own quiet determination; not necessarily by his skill on the field but by his steely approach off it. There are those who say Richard was unlucky not to captain England and it is known that it was a straight choice between him and Mike Brearley at one time. Brearley got the nod from the selectors and Gilliat's own career subsided, while Brearley's belatedly took off. It might so easily have been the other way round. Like Brearley, Gilliat was not a Test class batsman but he had many of the same leadership qualities and can count himself unlucky in that he achieved more domestically with a far weaker team.

Richards and I celebrated in the most positive fashion by tearing into Kent's attack, including Derek Underwood, at Southampton, each scoring centuries and helping Hampshire build up a total of 471 for 8, but Kent fought back well and the match was drawn, despite O'Sullivan taking another 5 wickets. O'Sullivan thus completed a truly fantastic personal month and was deservedly the hero of the hour. But before he had time to bask in the glory of his achievements, he received a letter in the post to say he had been sacked. We were all shocked and upset by his sacking, however unpalatable it may have been to the county themselves. Hampshire had an overseas vacancy for either O'Sullivan or the now qualified Andy Roberts. After much painful deliberation, they plumped for the sped of Roberts, reasoning that a spin bowler would be easier to replace. So Roberts, untried and raw in potential, was offered a contract and O'Sullivan was forced to leave. He was a sad and unhappy man as he reflected on the cruel twist at the moment of his greatest triumphs. He hardly spoke to anyone and what he did say was nothing more than a bitter succession of oaths. He went home to New Zealand soon soon afterwards and never returned to the county again.

In the one-day competitions, we again failed. We finished third in the John Player League and lasted only long enough in the others for me to set one record. At Amersham I scored an unbeaten 173 at a run a minute against the inadequate bowling attack of Minor Counties South in the Benson and Hedges Cup. It is still a record at the time of writing but the bowling was so easy that I scarcely list it among my great achievements. Looking back on it all, I see 1973 as my outstanding English season. It provided me with some of my best moments in county cricket and yet, because of the rejection by the West Indies, some of my worst feelings; a curious mixture to mark a season in which I came of age.

6 Clashes with Authority

By nature I am not an aggressive sort of person. You may find this difficult to believe by the way I strike a cricket ball, but what happens out there really has no bearing on the way I approach life in general. My wife and my friends will say that I am a man who prefers the company of a few people and would rather spend the evening at home than off on a tour of the night clubs. It had never occurred to me to question authority and, although I like to think I was prepared to stand up for what I considered to be my rights, I was always too easy-going ever to be much of a rebel. As a schoolboy and as a junior on the Hampshire staff I was taught that the word of the umpire was final and if I knew I was out I should assist him by walking. My early years in the county side did nothing to alter my attitude. Players accepted the umpire's signal without demur and there were opponents and team-mates alike who 'walked' without so much as a hint of reluctance. Nowadays, my attitude is regretfully very different and so too is that of many other professional cricketers. Some of the game's traditionalists will blame this on the amount of money being played for, others will say it merely reflects the changing values of society itself. Whatever the explanations, one thing is clear as far as I am concerned: I no longer walk until given out by the umpire. For this fundamental change I blame what happened to me and the rest of the West Indies touring team on what was billed as 'the clash of the century', the series against Australia in 1975–6. Australia were still smarting from their World Cup defeat in England in the summer at our hands and were desperate for revenge to restore national pride.

Dennis Amiss at first slip and wicket-keeper Derek Taylor watch the ball being hoisted over mid-wicket during a representative match

Test baptism in India. Prasanna of India bowled by Vanburn Holder. The fielders are (right to left) Richards, Murray, Kallicharran and Greenidge

Another six coming up . . . It was one of ten in this innings of 163 not out against Warwickshire in 1979 to set a new John Player League record. Phil Oliver is the bowler on the receiving end and the wicket-keeper is Chris Maynard (*Ken Kelly, Birmingham*)

Quite how desperate they were we did not realise until we got there in November of that year. I shall talk more about the tour later, but what happened there has since had a deep effect on me and the way I play cricket.

We felt, in short, we were cheated. Cheated by the Australian players and by the umpires. I shall never forget as long as I live how in the Fourth Test at Sydney Ian Chappell edged Michael Holding to Murray at the wicket when he had not scored. The entire team leapt for delight because Chappell's was a vital wicket by any standards. We heard the noise of bat touching ball and we saw the deviation. The umpire stood motionless and Chappell ignored all around him, pretending nothing had happened and preparing at his crease for the next delivery. Never have I been quite so astounded by a decision. Chappell was blatantly out and poor Holding, on his first tour, broke down and cried. Even the Aussie crowd, among whom impartiality is not a strong point, were embarrassed by the whole affair. Our morale crashed with that incident and although Chappell was soon out, we were never able to recover our composure and Australia won the Test, destroying the series as a contest. What it taught me was never to walk until the finger is raised. Ian Chappell is the worst culprit I have ever come across but there were a couple of incidents on that tour which reinforced my determination to do the same, particularly in Australia. Gary Cosier made himself a hero by coming into the Third Test at his Melbourne birthplace and scoring a century in his first innings. Yet twice we thought he was out before he had reached double figures. Twice umpire Bailhache turned down what we were certain were obvious lbws. Television supported our claims and, although I am the first to acknowledge that umpires must make an instant choice, we came to mistrust every decision Australian umpires made. Indeed after years of playing cricket in Australia I have come to the conclusion there is no such thing as a good Australian umpire.

Australians do not 'walk', it is as simple as that and since the umpires never get any help from the players, they err on the side of caution by refusing to give players out. No wonder Tom Brooks, one of the most senior of Australian match officials, gave up a beaten and bemused man after a Test match in which he was sworn at by Australia's Graeme Wood. In England I think the standard of umpiring is much better, although every county player in the country knows of the men who can be conned and occasionally fooled. I learned a lot from Ian Chappell that day in Sydney. He was the epitome of complete professionalism, while the West Indian players around him howled with rage and frustration. There was not the slightest hint of a guilty smile, not a trace of emotion in the tumult. While Holding hung his head, the tears streaming down his face, Chappell merely adjusted his pad, shifted his box and scratched his crease in readiness for the next ball. That single event, I believe, broke us as a team and won the series for the Australians.

I have to admit, having changed my attitude and refusing to go until given out, that on two occasions at least I have stayed my ground when I knew I was out and got away with it. Both times I got an edge when batting for Hampshire and had been 'caught' behind. I used the Chappell method, marked my crease and ignored the cries of anguish from the opposition. It is a trick of the trade now employed by many players. I am sorry to have to admit it but it would be dishonest of me now to pretend I have not done it. Indeed there have been times when I have played at a ball and genuinely not known whether I have touched it or not. When I first started I would have gone if I felt the appeals were strong enough, but not now. I remember Ian Chappell and wait for the umpire to make up his mind.

It may sound hypocritical, but I feel sorry for umpires. They have a difficult job and it is not made easier by players using gamesmanship. I have come to the conclusion that since so much is at stake in professional cricket, umpires should have some kind of physical examination before the start of the season. Certainly their eyes and ears should be tested because the demands on these faculties are now greater than ever. In my career I have been the victim of many decisions I considered wrong, mostly lbws, and there have been times when I have had a job to control my feelings.

70

Dissent is still the ultimate of cricket sins and I have heard it said that I have been seen to vent my feelings at a decision on the field. I must answer that by saying I have never shown dissent on the field—or at least only once! Sometimes it looks like anger at a decision if I beat the ground with my bat or even kick at the wickets. Such actions may seem childish but the 'dissent' is only disappointment or anger with myself, never fury at an umpire's decision, however bad it may seem. If, after hours of diligent concentration, I get out to a poor shot or because I made a fundamental error in technique, I am bitterly angry at myself, especially if I am near to a century. I think most umpires accept this and realise the mutterings and ground-beatings are not directed at them.

One umpire once thought otherwise and it almost cost me a reprimand from Lords. I was fresh back from the tour of 1974–5 in India and was playing in the relative peace of a county match at Bournemouth. David Evans was the umpire and he gave me out lbw when I thought I was well forward of my crease. I gave him a dirty look and departed in an obvious state of disagreement. I thought no more about it but my team-mates had noticed from the dressing room that Evans was equally unhappy at my response to his decision. A former Glamorgan wicketkeeper, he did not forget my action and at the end of play that day called into the dressing room and demanded to see Gilliat and myself. With the crowd long since gone and the prying eyes of the press out of the way, he led us to a little pathway behind the pavilion where, under the pines, he gave me a good lecture on my behaviour and warned Gilliat to make sure I never did it again. The folly of my dissent was brought home to me when Evans threatened to take the matter further and report me to the authorities at Lords but we managed to get him to change his mind. It was a lucky escape and one from which I learned a lot.

Of the umpires around the world, there are a few in whom I have complete confidence, but only a few. In my opinion Dicky Bird is the best in the world and I think Barrie Meyer is not far behind. Outside England, Douglas Sang Hue of Jamaica is the one

71

to impress me most, but, call it bias from a bitter failure, but other West Indians—and many Englishmen—will confirm that there is no such thing as a good Australian umpire. I suppose any kind of criticism of umpires sounds like sour grapes and I'm well aware every player has been given out by dubious decisions for as long as there has been cricket. All I am saying is that, in the nine or ten years I have been playing cricket at the top level, attitudes have changed among the players and it is the umpires who have had to suffer. It was the experience of Australia which taught me I had to change because I saw that in opponents it was successful to cheat. My outlook hardened when it became apparent my opponents would not budge unless the stumps were knocked out of the ground and now, like them, I wait for the poor old umpire's signal, even if I realise I'm out. I know it's sad, but it is just a question of survival.

Most cricketers have found the pressures of all kinds have become intense in the last few years and what used to be a gentle game is now as competitive as any other big-money sport. Counties need to be successful on the field to increase gate money and membership; players need to be in the first team in order to earn a cap and to be in line for any bonus-money share-out. Gone are the days when counties were supported by generous donations from wealthy patrons and when equally wealthy players performed for fun alone. I do not regret the increasing commercialism and, as a family man, the money is of prime consideration. For that reason, I mourn the passing of Kerry Packer's World Series Cricket. Not only is the series as competitive as any conventional tour but it also provided the sort of rewards about which players like myself had only dreamed before. Financial security is a worry which plagues all professional cricketers at whatever level and in the prevailing commercial climate, we all feel entitled to make demands which a few years ago would have seemed prohibitive. The days of the amateur are long gone and, however much that may be regretted by some, the facts indicate that nowadays players are in the game to make a living. Cricket must now pay its way and it is the duty of the administrators to bring in as much money as possible. If nothing else, the Kerry Packer affair will have made the public aware how poorly paid cricketers have been in the past and, in my view, it is no coincidence that the 'average' county cricketer, who was so vehemently against Packer at one time, now enjoys a salary of £4,250 a year as compared with £3,000 two years ago. Try telling me that Packer was not indirectly responsible.

Cricket is all about pressure these days and each type of competition produces its own demands. For instance, I do not think there are any fewer pressures playing for Hampshire than for the West Indies. If anything, the necessity for me to do well for Hampshire is greater than it is for the West Indies. Of course I am expected to make a contribution when opening for the West Indies but, and I hope I do not sound too arrogant when I say this, it is vital for me to score runs regularly for my county in our present position. I have had to change my natural game in the last year or so on the county circuit because it has been desperately important for me not to get out. This means I have been forced to resist the temptation of hitting every ball in the manner I would like. The change in style does not apply all the time but I feel now I have to score runs for Hampshire which puts me under greater pressure than is fair. Sometimes I have been trying too hard and promptly getting out. There have been times also when I have worked myself up into a panic under the impression that I have to do well. Hampshire have a frail batting line-up, now that people like Richards, Gilliat and Sainsbury have gone and there is the thought, however misplaced, that if I do not make a big innings then no one will. This may reflect badly on Turner and Jesty and others, but it is not meant to be a criticism of men with whom I have virtually grown up. However, in the last year or two I have felt the increasing necessity to do well at all costs. For the West Indies, the pressures are almost as great but totally different.

Television, big crowds and the constant attention of the press all make it a world apart from the county game but the worries are still there. My first desire is to get enough runs to keep my international place and then to get the West Indies total on to a sound footing. I am always aware that if I do not get runs for the West Indies, they will soon find someone else who will. Desmond

73

Haynes has sprung to prominence quickly and I may have been fortunate in that he slotted neatly into the hole vacated by Roy Fredericks, otherwise I might even have lost my place. There is no real security in Test cricket and having been dropped once or twice before, I am conscious of how transitory life at the highest level can be. A touch of insecurity can certainly prevent complacency and a sharp desire for runs ensures a continued ride on the gravy-train. I should say what a change it makes to play in a side as powerful as the West Indies after the struggles in recent years with Hampshire. It is a matter of pride in my personal performance to open the West Indies score with a healthy contribution and it is no real consolation to know that if I fail there are so many brilliant players still to bat. If anything, the presence of Viv Richards, Kallicharran, Lloyd, Lawrence Rowe and all the others acts as a spur and forces me to get enough runs to be counted among their equals. As such, there is great personal rivalry between the different members of the West Indian team although I expect many of them would not be prepared to admit it.

My approach to any match is dictated by what kind of a competition it is. Obviously if it's a one-day match then I will try to play in a different way from a five-day Test match. I have one basic, over-riding philosophy and that's to hit the ball as hard as possible. It may sound facile, but not every player does hit the ball as hard as he can. I figure that as long as I hit the ball with all my power I will get runs. Time after time in my career I have been dropped because I have hit the ball so powerfully that the fielder simply could not hold it. In other words, as long as I continue with my policy, I will always stand a chance of getting away with even miscued shots. As an opener I am on the receiving end of a hard, red missile being hurled at me at something like 90–100 miles an hour. I have a split second in which to play it. Sometimes it thuds into my body and anyone who has been struck by a cricket ball will know exactly how painful it can be. I try never to show the extreme pain it causes but there have been times when, next day, I have been unable to move my limbs because they are covered by a mass of excruciating bruises. I hit the ball, therefore, as a form of

74

revenge, a personal vendetta against the ball. When I smite it into the distance I think back to all the pain I have been caused and vow to do the same again as soon as possible. So, if you have ever wondered what I am thinking when they are looking for a ball which I have just struck for six, now you know. It is revenge; sweet, sweet revenge.

In Test matches, my first job is to stay there and take the shine off the new ball. If, after an hour I am still at the crease, then I start to think in terms of picking up runs. That's the theory anyway, but it does not often work out like that.

Instinctively I will hit the first ball of a Test match for six if I realise in that split second it can be done. What's more, if the bowling is poor in the first hour then I will attack it. Maybe I am alone in this attitude, but think back to the number of Test matches where bad bowling in the early part of a Test match has gone unpunished because the batsman has not had the confidence to attack so early. England in recent years have only had Colin Milburn and, to a lesser extent, John Jameson ready to take a Test attack apart from the start. Milburn was devastatingly successful because he was prepared to take the chance and have a go at poor bowling. Does it mean that since his premature departure there has been no poor bowling from new-ball attacks? I am inclined to the Milburn philosophy: if the bowling is bad, attack it whatever the status of the match. Having said all that, I am conscious of the need to build big innings, to build the solid foundations of a team score of worthwhile proportions. In one-day matches, be it the World Cup or a humble John Player League game, I try to score off every ball. It's not as difficult as it sounds because fields are defensive and there are acres of empty space through the often unattended slip area and if I succeed for long enough, the initiative soon shifts away from the bowling side. I have a stack of medals and awards as a result of this theory and, even if they are all eventually overhauled, batting records simultaneously held in the John Player League, the Benson and Hedges Cup and in the Gillette Cup. I think I can say without undue conceit that my policy has been successful.

After ten years as an opening batsman I am firmly convinced I would hate to bat anywhere else. It seems curious to recall that it needed an emergency way back in 1970 to thrust me into a position for which I am now internationally renowned. Yet once I became an opener, there was never any doubt it was my best position in the batting order. To be honest I cannot stand batting lower in the order. I get nervous, edgy and very unpleasant company when I am forced for one reason or another to come in lower down. Batting at Test level is a nerve-racking business at the best of times but over the years I have learned to overcome the nerves with a few quiet moments on my own before stepping out to the wicket. As an opener, I do not have time to get too worked up, but I admit to getting terribly nervous and impatient watching others in the knowledge that my turn is yet to come. If I am due to come in at three or four, I get so nervous that I end up hoping my team-mates are out quickly so I can get out there and start playing. Sounds a little selfish, but it's true. Once the early overs are safely negotiated I find my nerves quickly evaporate and I am able to concentrate on building an innings. But the nerves soon return when I approach the magic 100. Like many players I am never conscious of the scoreboard, apart from the occasional glance, but once I get near the 90s I grab each run as if it was my last. There is no worse feeling in cricket, apart from a 'King Pair', than being out just a few short of a century. I have been out in the 90s more times than I care to remember, more often through my own lack of conviction than anything produced by the bowler. It is the most awful feeling.

When you return to the pavilion a few disappointing runs short of a ton, you start thinking of all the singles unaccepted and the fours stopped just inches away from the boundary—but I find talking about the 'nervous 90s' so distressing, I shall discontinue the topic!

Cricket may not be the leisurely pursuit of old but it does offer some moments when the pressure is off and the players can relax. Over the years at Hampshire we have found ways of keeping ourselves amused, particularly when fielding. Barry Richards, John Rice, wicketkeeper Bob Stephenson and myself have all taken our close-to-the-wicket jobs seriously, but to pass the long hours in the field we have been known to let our attention wander every now and then and to think of other things. Some county matches become so unbelievably boring that we start setting each other puzzles and working out anagrams—anything to relieve the tedium of the day's cricket. 'I spy' is a favourite pastime of the Hampshire slips, so if you see a lot of Hampshire fielders looking around aimlessly during a particularly monotonous period of play, you know what we are doing. All this, of course, puts pressure on the captains to make sure concentration is maintained at 100 per cent. There's no such time to relax during a Test match but Clive Lloyd occasionally has to remind us to pay attention. Captaincy is not an easy task and some great players make ordinary skippers. Roy Marshall springs to mind as one who failed to become as great a captain as he was a player. It is my opinion alone, but I do not think Clive will go down in history as one of the game's inspirational leaders. Clive, a marvellous and instinctive cricketer, was the captain of a great team or potentially a great team. I mean no criticism of him when I say that a more natural leader could have turned us into the most outstanding of all post-war teams, although we have since come preciously near it after our 2–0 win in Australia in 1979–80.

When we were losing so heavily and so disappointingly in Australia in 1975–6, Lloyd found it impossible to lift us individually or collectively and was as bemused and shattered as the rest of us when Australia went on to win 5–1 with as much ease as the scoreline suggests. There have been times when the West Indies have been doing well when an old-age pensioner could captain us. All the skipper needs to do when we are all getting runs is to do the obvious and maintain the momentum. This Clive did, but I can think of few real instances when this shrewd leadership changed the course of a match. I believe Tony Greig has never been given the credit he deserves for his qualities as captain. He was a fairly ordinary player but a great competitor and always appeared to get the best out of limited resources as skipper of England in the mid-70s. Mike Brearley is universally respected for his captaincy but I do not think Lloyd ranks with either of them as a captain, though he was a better player than the pair of them put together. Clive did not always get the support he warranted from the West Indies Board of Control, nor from the various managers. Deryck Murray has helped Clive on the field enormously, as I'm sure he would be the first to acknowledge. Deryck might even have made a better skipper but overall, I feel Clive has not done a bad job and there have been many occasions when I have been glad not to be in his shoes. It is easy to captain a winning side; the measure of a real skipper is his ability to motivate a losing one. Clive was not always able to do this. Richard Gilliat got the best out of moderate players and for that he earned our respect.

I hope that some captain gets the best out of the young Kent and England fast bowler Graham Dilley because I believe he can become one of England's best discoveries for some years. He has the potential to be an outstanding player. I have only played against him a handful of times but quickly realised he was going to be a real force one day. His length and line are awkward to handle. He bowls wide of the crease but still makes it leave the right-hander and, with his height, is a very difficult customer! Around the counties there are many players I respect, although I like to think there is no one bowler whom I hate to face. Mike Hendrick is one whom I do not always relish and John Lever is for ever doing something intelligent. Phil Edmonds has done well for England but I could not understand the fury engendered by the selection of Derek Underwood instead of him for the 1979–80 tour of Australia. For me Underwood is the master. We have had some rare old tussles over the years. No batsman ever gets the better of him for long and there are times when it becomes impossible to score runs from him. Most players end up where they deserve but probably because I know him better than most, I have often felt Trevor Jesty was unlucky to be ignored by the English selectors. Jesty strikes the ball as cleanly and as smoothly as any player in the world but it took him ten years to get a century and only now is he beginning to realise his own vast potential. The nearest he got to selection was a Test trial and as an official stand-by for the England tour to Pakistan and New Zealand. Trevor is an example of what mind cannot do over matter. He got it into his head that inferior players were in the England team and he sank into a mire of worry and doubt all of his own making. Trevor failed to get runs consistently and, for all his ability, will probably never play for his country. A great shame.

7 Caribbean Nightmare

Hampshire's championship success of 1973 and my own huge leap forward as a batsman led to another invitation from Barbados to spend the winter there playing for them in the Shell Shield. After my previous unhappy season with them I was not sure of receiving this second chance to prove my worth on the parched and bone-hard wickets of the West Indies. My feelings were a little mixed as I read of the invitation. In one respect it vindicated my decision not to throw in my lot with England because the selectors obviously wanted another chance to measure my improvement, but at the same time I was filled with trepidation about returning to such an environment so personally hostile towards me. Would I still be subject to that terrible abuse? Would walking out at the Kensington Oval still be such a desperate ordeal? And would things have changed sufficiently for me to break through and win over the confidence of our volatile supporters? These were questions which worried me deeply before I decided to take a chance and return. To be honest, there were not many alternative ways of spending the English close-season and the prospect of going back to the production line of some big factory acted as all the incentive I needed to return and try again in Barbados. Having failed once out there in my native island, I felt duty bound to show them all I had become a player worthy of consideration at the highest level. Banks Brewery offered me a job again and, with a flat lined up in St Michael's, I set off for Bridgetown determined to make amends for the disasters of the previous winter. The Barbados board of control paid my fare again and I arrived home with a burning desire to set the record straight. As you will recall, it was not the first time in my life when I had had so much to prove to so many.

I only wish I could say that I succeeded. Far from it. Another six matches for Barbados in the inter-island shield and another disappointing return for my efforts. Working for the brewery was both enjoyable and not very strenuous. Thanks to the generosity of the manager, Ian Clarke, there was plenty of time for practice and for playing in club and representative matches and there was no earthly reason, from the preparation point of view, why I should have failed again. After a summer in England I had forgotten how the glare made my eyes water, how I was forced to squint with 'tears' rolling down my cheeks while batting, and how the extra bounce accounted for my wicket with monotonous regularity. I was playing the same shots which brought me runs by the bucket ful in England and instead of the ball crashing into the fence, I was edging the ball firmly into the hands of the wicketkeeper or slips. I did not have the experience to make allowances and my desire to get a big score under my belt for Barbados led to my abandoning caution and attacking every possible ball. In England I most certainly have got away with it but a succession of comparatively low scores sent my confidence and morale crashing to rock bottom. My return from eleven innings was 353 runs at an average of just under 40. On paper it does not look too bad but in fact that total was smaller than the previous Barbadian winter and I was not satisfied. What's more, it was the second season for them in which I failed to score a century. To my intense irritation I got as far as 90 in one match before getting out. All of which merely added fuel to the fury of my many personal barrackers who carried on their hate campaign every bit as virulently as before. I could hear them screaming for my blood every time I went out to bat and every failure was greeted with the familiar 'Go home, Englishman' from the howling mobs clawing at the wire around boundaries from one end of the West Indies to the other.

Only two fifties in the eleven innings scarcely represented a major achievement and for that reason I was surprised and pleased to be asked to play for the West Indies Board of Control President's XI again, this time against the English tourists at the Kensington Oval. I had not really expected to be chosen on my results and it gave me another good opportunity to use the occasion to further my Test chances in a match which was only one step below a proper international. The fact that it was being played at Kensington caused me a few problems because there was always the fear of failure in front of my own fans, and how they would have loved that! All the pre-match publicity suggested this was to be a trial for me but the pressure was doubled when I heard it said that I was the key man to the outcome of the match. The pundits reckoned that since I faced English bowlers all the time playing for Hampshire then I should be able to get plenty of runs against them out here. Not unnaturally, I was amazed by their reasoning but it did nothing for my peace of mind. Supposing the West Indies selectors were thinking the same thing?

I went out to bat to the roars of a large and vociferous crowd to face the attack which included fast bowler Bob Willis. Willis, tall and angular, pitched one short at me. I saw it in plenty of time and went to pull it. Unfortunately I missed it completely and was dealt a sickening blow in the 'box'. I collapsed to the floor, writhing in pain as the crowd jeered ironically. I was just about unconscious by the time I was led from the field and on the way back to the pavilion I vomited through my gloves, such was my distress. The crowd, lifted equally by drink and excitement, thought it all amusing enough to continue their jibes as I made my shaky way back to the dressing room. For hours afterwards I lay slumped on a couch with a severe headache and stomach pains which have never equalled in intensity either before or since. I think I wished I was dead.

Much as I enjoy Barbados, the sunshine, the easy atmosphere and returning to my relatives, I found it tough coming to terms with cricketing life out there. Two full seasons and not a big score worthy of mention filled me with the fear that I might not be asked back for a third time. The injury in the most vital of matches only added to my apprehension and once again I returned to England with a certain amount of relief. The West Indies had a tour of India, Pakistan and Sri Lanka looming on the horizon for the winter of 1974–5 and from what I could work out, there were plenty of places going begging for anyone capable of nudging the selectors with a series of big scores. I was luckier in that respect than the home-based players who had no competition between now and the tour in which to reaffirm their ability. They could rely on reputation alone while I at least had a full summer with Hampshire in which to show the selectors that my form of 1973 was no flash in the pan.

Having won the championship so decisively the previous summer, indeed without losing a game, the mood was decidedly buoyant when the players reassembled for 1974. O'Sullivan had gone but the pace of Andy Roberts was now available as a new and potent weapon in our armoury with which to try to retain the title. Our story of 1974 is one of the all-time hard luck stories in the history of the county championship. We lost our title by two points to Worcestershire after unseasonal rain at Bournemouth at the height of the holiday period had washed out our last two matches. The final margin of 227 to 225 turned the whole summer sour for us, especially as, had rain not intervened, we would almost certainly have retained the championship.

After fifteen matches, something like three-quarters of the season gone, we were handily poised to go on and win for the second successive year. We led Worcestershire, our only real rivals at this stage, by 31 points (197–166) and unless we simply lost our nerve and surrendered abjectly in our remaining matches, I think it fair to say that it would have needed a miracle to stop us. Either a miracle or divine intervention. It seems it was one of the two which swung the race Worcestershire's way when they must surely have given up hope of catching up. It came as a bitter blow for us all in the Hampshire camp when our match with Yorkshire at Dean Park was washed out and news filtered through that Worcestershire had gleaned enough bonus points to deny us the county championship. What made it all the more sickening was the knowledge that when we played against Worcestershire earlier in the summer we had beaten them by an innings. However, I am not prepared to complain perhaps as much as some of my colleagues. Looking back, I am not prepared to blame the weather for our failure, although no one can deny that it was the rain which finally overcame us. I believe we should have wrapped it all up long before we came to Bournemouth for the last two matches. We still had a good side and Andy Roberts made us into a formidable one; we were the side best equipped to win the title for a second time because, unlike so many other counties, we were never affected by Test calls. Teams such as Kent and Warwickshire were almost continually playing reserves because the selectors of more than one country were using their players. No one so much as looked at any of our players and we were able to stay as a unit for virtually the entire year.

Andy Roberts made a big difference to us. His speed and his intelligence saw him run through some of the finest batting orders in the country, demolishing top batsmen like skittles and ending the season with an outstanding haul of 119 wickets at little over 13 each. Andy came from Antigua and emerged from that island at the same time as Viv Richards. The pair of them came over to Alf Gover's coaching school in London and it was from there that Hampshire persuaded him to try his luck in county cricket. Like me, Andy saw the possibilities of an early break into international competition if he could produce the results, and playing for Hampshire seemed to him a lucrative way of gaining experience. His huge tally of wickets won him instant respect up and down England and a quick passport to the Test team. In his own quiet way, he was a very determined man and never more so than when he first came into the county team in the controversial circumstances of O'Sullivan's leaving and with Hampshire pinning so much faith on him. Gilliat used his new pace bowler more than he should have done in 1974 as his 727 overs will testify, but at the time Andy was happy enough just to be making a contribution and his tremendous success induced him to keep going even when he felt tired and in need of a rest. In later years, of course, he rebelled and left mid-way through the 1978 season, accused of all sorts of things he did not really deserve.

Andy was labelled a Black Power agitator, a dressing-room rebel, and idle and anti-establishment. I shared a flat with Andy

Anita Greenidge. Anita, an Antiguan raised in London, was a typist in the City of London when I met her. We married in Walthamstow, London in September 1977

Father and son. Gordon and Carl take time off to pose for the cameras. Carl was born in 1978 and is already a seasoned traveller and cricket-watcher

and after I got married, he lived with my wife and me until he left the club. I suppose I know him as well as anyone but having said that, I cannot really claim to be a particularly close friend. I even married one of his cousins and he and I have been colleagues on several tours and room-mates during away matches for Hampshire.

In spite of the impression he may have given, Andy was always keen to do well for Hampshire or for whoever else he may have been playing, although he kept his own counsel. Indeed in all the time we shared a flat we hardly ever spoke to each other. He might just as well have been living somewhere else. For one whole summer at a flat near Southampton's football ground, we did not say so much as a 'hello'. The only time he ever said anything to me was if he wanted a lift into the city centre. For the rest of the time he lived in his own world of soul and reggae music and emerged only to play cricket. Don't get the impression that he had nothing to offer. He was keen to do his bit for the club but when he was injured all he could think about was resting. He once told me that too many fast bowlers lost their sting because they were over-bowled and he was determined not to let it happen to him. Gilliat did use him too much and when the injuries started to occur, Andy saw the warning lights. The matter came to a head when we played Warwickshire at Edgbaston one year. Andy had been bowling for a long time and Gilliat, who had been sensing a breakthrough, threw the ball to him to start another over. He wanted him to keep up the attack although Andy, by his standards, had not been bowling well. Andy felt he had had enough and promptly threw the ball back to the skipper. The Hampshire players watched in stunned silence. Gilliat had two alternatives. Either he insisted Andy carried on or he gave way and allowed him the rest he so obviously desired. Andy started to walk down to fine-leg, as I remember, and Gilliat realised there was no point in making a scene and let it pass. By now the Warwickshire crowd were sensing something had gone wrong and there was a groundswell of jeering as Hampshire tried to sort out their internal problems in the full face of the public. It must have looked bad and I know Gilliat more than once lectured Andy after this incident, but by then his resolve had gone. Andy saw it all as a matter of principle. He was quite prepared to play, but as a fast bowler, not to bowl himself into the ground and into premature retirement.

For all the comments laid against him about his politics, I honestly do not think he was ever anti-white. He was aware of West Indian history as I am, and I think above all his main concern is the dignity of the blacks and the need for the West Indians to retain their separate culture. Some of the people with whom he consorted in England were more politically motivated and I think it was because he spent his spare time with them that he aroused the suspicions of a cricketing public which tends anyway to shy away from political realities. Hunched and unsmiling, he may have given the wrong impression to cricket lovers all over the world. In fact, he has a fine, dry sense of humour and is quite prepared to join in the sarcastic banter of any dressing-room, particularly at Hampshire where he and Jesty were always trying to goad each other. On this day, he is still as shrewd and as cunning as any fast bowler in the world—almost the equal of Lillee in that respect without having the same perpetually hostile approach. This is going to sound strange, but I believe there was one ultimate reason why he walked out of county cricket and retreated to Antigua. It was the English cold. Having been born and bred in the warmth of the West Indies he never came to terms with the chill of an English summer and my memories of him in England always have him swathed in jumpers. In the end, and 1978 was a poor summer for weather, it got too much for him. The cold and the wet got to his bones and rather than put up with it any longer, he gave up a healthy contract and returned to the Caribbean. Nowadays I venture to suggest that Roberts is no longer the West Indies main strike bowler; Holding has long since superseded him. Now Garner and Croft have emerged as lethal fast bowlers, young enough to be filled with ambition and I believe Andy may soon have to fight for his test place.

I don't wish to sound jealous, but I have always felt Roberts and his Antiguan compatriot Viv Richards have been lucky in that ever since they came to prominence as juniors their way has been carefully paved for them. The pair were sent over on a scholarship to Alf Gover's school, where counties were alerted to their potential and duly signed them. I have often wondered if my life would have been easier had I been bred and discovered on one of the Caribbean islands. The kids may not have outstanding wickets to play on, but if they show any talent at all, there is enough collective knowledge in the form of old players and coaches to make sure they are promoted quickly through the various stages. I am the only member of the West Indies party who has come to the top via another route and there are still moments when I feel like an outsider in the West Indies dressing room.

But in 1974 any kind of international recognition seemed a long way off as I set about building on the personal success of the previous summer and trying to eradicate the minor disasters of the previous winter. I wish I could say the championship season of 1974 was as good to me as the year in which we won the title. Hampshire, of course, came desperately close to winning it again but for my own part it was something of a disappointment and my critics might have been justified in thinking I had regressed a little. Indeed it needed an extraordinary innings of 273 not out for Derrick Robins's XI against the Pakistanis at Eastbourne near the end of the season to see me past 1,000 runs for the season. For Hampshire, though, I was well down in the averages with only one century in 31 innings and only 804 runs to show for a summer's graft. I think I might reasonably have expected another 400 or 500 runs, which might have been enough to put the championship safely in our grasp.

I was making decent starts to an innings but, as so often in the past, getting out when I should have been going on to make big scores. My attacking methods have often been my undoing and I have often contemplated grafting like Geoff Boycott for century after century. But don't worry, there's no chance of that.

There was no hint of the mediocre season to come when I began 1974 in fine style with a century in my first knock of the championship year against Middlesex at Lords. I scored 13 fours and a six in making 120 and there was nothing to suggest that it would not be the first of many. I could not repeat the dose in the second innings and we slumped to a 100 run defeat, our first in the championship since August 1972.

Collectively, it did not take us long to come to our senses and to string together enough wins to re-establish ourselves as a force in the title race. The first real hint of our power came on the uncertain wicket of the pretty little club ground at Basingstoke. We were playing Kent who, for once, had their full contingent of Test players of all nationalities in action. Against Bernard Julien, John Shepherd and Derek Underwood we did well to reach 290 for 9 before declaring, after England skipper Mike Denness had put us in. What happened after that is little short of sensational. Roberts, firing for the first time, ripped through their batting with the aid of Bob Herman and Mike Taylor and they were all out for 86. It was this, the second day of the match, which served notice upon the cricketing world that in Roberts, a new and exciting power had emerged. The reason for this was not necessarily his figures of 4 for 12. Poor Colin Cowdrey, one of the game's great names, knows exactly why. Andy let loose a delivery which completely beat Cowdrey for sheer pace and struck him a nasty blow on the head. Cowdrey collapsed on to his wicket and there were pictures next day in the papers of him pole-axed surrounded by sympathetic Hampshire players—all except, that is Roberts, who stood impatiently 10 yards away waiting for the next batsman. A shiver of fear must have run up the backs of just about every county batsman in the country.

Roberts did even better in the second innings (5 for 27) and without Cowdrey, Kent were all out for a second time just before tea on the second day to give us victory by an innings and 71. Never have I seen a group of Test players (nine of them capped) leave a county ground in such a hurry. The win over Kent was the first of five by us inside two days during the season and it seems incredible to recall that we still failed to win the championship. Andy was equally devastating in our next match at Chelmsford where he took 9 more wickets to help us beat Essex by an innings and 16 runs. Turner and Gilliat got centuries but my contribution was a nought. I fared little better in our next two matches at Trent Bridge and at Bournemouth where we met Sussex. Barry Richards scored 225 against Nottinghamshire and we won in two days and against Sussex, Bob Herman, benefiting from having Roberts at the other end, took 9 wickets in the match to crush our local rivals in two days also.

By now, we were well into June and topping the table. The spate of easy wins continued unabated: a second demolition of Kent, this time at Tunbridge Wells; a 6 wicket win over Leicestershire at Portsmouth; and a 9 wicket defeat of Gloucestershire at Southampton. Sussex got their revenge in the middle of July at Hove but big wins over Northamptonshire and Warwickshire restored us to the top and boosted our confidence for the all-important month of August. My own contribution to these victories was far from startling and only the occasional brisk fifty served notice that I had something to offer. With August now upon us, Hampshire needed me to come up with something special to sustain the impetus. On the whole, I failed.

Our severest test came early in the month at Portsmouth where our nearest rivals in the race, Worcestershire, were the visitors. There was a big crowd who anticipated that the winners of this match would go on to become the champions. Norman Gifford, the Worcestershire captain, chose to bat first but our seam attack shared the wickets between them and they were all out for 94, their lowest total of the season. Unfortunately I had made only 3 when I was out, but Gilliat inspired Hampshire to build a first innings lead of 142. Roberts and Herman ran through them a second time for less than a hundred and it was all over just about an hour before the scheduled close of the second day. Surely, nothing could stop us now. Thirty-one points in the lead and only five matches to play. Only rain could prevent us winning the title again. It did. At Bournemouth in the next match, there was enough rain to allow Lancashire to hold on for a draw which in all probability they would not have done in normal circumstances. More rain at Cardiff caught us on a drying wicket after building a big first innings lead over Glamorgan and the Welsh county took advantage of it to recover and best us. So to Southampton and more rain for the return game with Glamorgan over August Bank Holiday. Turner and Richards scored centuries in a big first innings total for us and Glamorgan must have been glad that only 15 minutes play was possible on the second day. We went into the third day needing to take 17 Glamorgan wickets to win. We took the first 7 of them without much bother and Glamorgan were forced to follow on 237 behind and half a day in which to stop us. The score was 51 for 2 with fewer than 20 overs left. Our task seemed hopeless, but Bob Herman produced an inspired spell of bowling to take 6 wickets for 2 runs in 7 overs. The atmosphere was incredible as fielders clustered around the bat in a last, desperate effort to clinch this most unlikely of victories.

Arthur Francis and Barry Lloyd hung on grimly for all our efforts and at 81 for 8, they survived five torrid overs to hold on for a draw. Had we won then, I'm sure the rain at Bournemouth in our last two matches would not have mattered. As it was, we went down to Bournemouth Week with Worcestershire rapidly closing the gap and with hints of desperation creeping in. We were still confident, though, of ultimate victory, providing the August rains finally disappeared and gave us six days of the sort of sunshine expected of a holiday resort at the height of the summer. In the first of our matches, against Somerset, we built up a huge 405 for 9 without much help from me and Brian Close's team began their second innings 141 behind. At 90 for 4 at the close of play on the second day, Somerset could not have expected anything other than defeat on the final day. But during the night the rains returned and no play was possible. The mood in the dressing room was one of intense frustration and irritation. We could do nothing but sit around searching the skies for hints of sunshine and a break in the blackness which surrounded Dean Park. Thus we went into our last match of the season against Yorkshire with a lead whittled down to two points by a Worcestershire side belatedly sensing their chance.

More rain washed out any chance of play in the entire match. The groundstaff worked miracles trying to get the match under way but their efforts were in vain, and not a ball was bowled. As we played cards, read papers and talked solemnly among ourselves, Worcestershire were able to start their match against Essex. Gifford won the toss, put Essex in and bowled them out, so giving his team enough bonus points to go into the lead. No further play was possible at Chelmsford and with us unable to even get started at Bournemouth, these bonus points were sufficient to give Worcestershire the title. We were heart-broken by the whole affair. Six victories by an innings and we were merely runners-up. We might just as well have finished last.

My personal season was redeemed by the most remarkable innings of my life at Eastbourne late in July. With Barry Richards I was selected to play for Derrick Robins's XI against the Pakistani tourists at the pretty little Saffrons ground. The match itself had no particular significance and Mr Robins always made sure the hospitality was good for such games played under his auspices. Pakistan had just finished playing in a Test match at Headingley the previous day and had travelled the 300 miles or so south after the match. Barry and I travelled together, arriving at a hotel outside Eastbourne at around midnight. We were both tired after the trip but there was a big steak meal awaiting us and plenty to drink. I was hungry as well, and quickly made light of the food. Unfortunately, I must have drunk far too much lager and when finally I staggered up to bed at around two o'clock I was feeling bloated and not a little happy. Five hours later I woke up with the most dreadful hangover, although I really had no idea exactly how much I had drunk. I stared out on to the countryside with my head spinning around with the most dreadful feeling of nausea. The mere thought of breakfast was too awful to contemplate and I figured the only way to sober up in time for the start of play was to have a shower. I stuck my head under the shower and I must have been there for an hour or more in a desperate attempt to banish the misery of the hangover. But when I emerged back in to the daylight, the headache and shakes were still with me and I was beginning to panic in the knowledge that I was going to let down so many people in playing in my state. Pakistan included several of

93

their top-line players and I politely asked to bat at number three in the hope that a nice opening stand would give me a chance to recover.

As Barry and his opening partner Neal Abberley of Warwickshire went out to bat to a polite ripple of applause, I was grappling with my pads, my gloves and my head. Of course, just when I wanted two men to stay out there, Richards was out and I was told it was my turn. I figured it would all be over blessedly quickly and I could return to the pavilion and recover in some dark corner. I reached the wicket with my head still spinning in circles and feeling like death. What happened then, I really have no recollection. I batted purely from instinct, hitting every ball with a ferocity unmatched by any other innings that I have played either before or since. I was determined to hammer everything in sight if only to justify the hospitality of my hosts. Any moment I expected my wicket to be shattered, but it never happened. Everything came right for some completely unknown reason. I middled every ball and yet hardly saw one delivery clearly. Every shot evaded fielders I had not seen and not at any stage during the day could I have told you if the bowler was left-arm fast or right-arm googly. I cannot remember a single shot but when I returned to the pavilion, rather later than I had anticipated, I discovered I had made 273 not out. Until then I had not got a clue how many I had made. The facts tell me I hit 13 sixes and 31 fours but I am hard pushed to remember a single boundary. All I ever recall of that day was my pounding head, my dry throat and a sort of numbness. It was, of course, a career-best score and I doubt if I shall ever get near it again. Perhaps I should get drunk more often. Joking aside, it earned me a few headlines and must have gone some way to assuring the West Indian selectors that I was capable of playing a big innings against Test class opposition. It was as well they never discovered the circumstances of my achievement.

It was also during 1974 that I met my wife, Anita. She is an Antiguan who came to this country when she was seven. As a cousin of Andy Roberts, she had come down with a coachload of Antiguans to see Andy and Viv Richards play against each other.

Of course, it would have to rain and they never did get to see them in action. Anita was friendly with a girl with whom Andy was going out, and at his suggestion we drove in my car to spend the rest of a wet day at an amusement fair at Southsea in Portsmouth. I got to know and like her that day, although at the time she was going out with someone else. I wrote to her occasionally after we met but it was not until nearly two years later that I plucked up enough courage to ask her to marry me. Anita, a shorthand typist with a firm of engineers in the City of London, married me in Walthamstow in September 1977. Now we have a son, Carl, and live in the outskirts of Southampton at Chandlers Ford in a bungalow which cost me £15,000, on which I had a considerable mortgage.

At our wedding there were something like 500 people, 150 more than we had expected. It was good to see among the stunningly large crowds Clive Lloyd, Roberts, John Holder, John Rice from Hampshire, and the man to whom I owed so much—Arthur Holt —not least for lending me his pyjamas all those years back.

8 Test Match Baptism

The West Indies tour to India, Pakistan and Sri Lanka, scheduled for the winter of 1974–5, was occupying my mind during the closing weeks of the domestic season of 1974. I had worked out all the permutations and I reckoned I had a better than even chance of making it. The trouble was that although Hampshire's achievements of 1973 and my part in them had put me on top of the world, the next summer had been a disappointment by my own increasingly demanding standards. If it had not been for that huge double hundred against the Pakistanis, I would not have reached 1,000 for the season and only one championship century represented a setback in my career which had shown continued improvements for four years. I began to think that my failures both in Barbados and in England might count against me when the selectors sat down to choose a tour party. I had learned already not to count chickens, so the announcement that I was in a seventeen-man squad came as the best news of my career so far. In hindsight, it is still one of the great moments.

It was very much an inexperienced West Indian side which assembled for the tour. There was no Sobers and no Kanhai, two of the great names of the past. Only the great spin bowler Lance Gibbs remained of the old guard and in Roberts, Richards and myself they were choosing players who had really only ever delivered the goods in English cricket. Yet we were supposed to become the backbone of the next generation of West Indian teams. Clive Lloyd was skipper, the Trinidad wicketkeeper Deryck Murray was his vice-captain and the party was loaded heavily with spinners of whom—other than Gibbs—were known outside the West Indies. The other front-line spin specialists were Albert

Padmore, groomed for so long as Gibbs's successor, Arthur Barrett, who had done so well for Jamaica, and the slow-left-arm variation of Elquemedo Willett. In addition, Roy Fredericks bowled occasional leg-spin and Viv Richards's off-spin had had moments of success.

The tour was to take four months and included five Tests against India, two against Pakistan and three matches in Sri Lanka. Not having toured before, I had no idea how tough such an itinerary can be and it was only afterwards that I realised just how long four months can seem. The party was Clive Lloyd (Guyana, captain), Deryck Murray (Trinidad, vice-captain), Len Baichan (Guyana), Arthur Barrett (Jamaica), Keith Boyce (Barbados), Roy Fredericks (Guyana), Lance Gibbs (Guyana), Gordon Greenidge (Barbados), Vanburn Holder (Barbados), Bernard Julien (Trinidad), Alvin Kallicharran (Guyana), David Murray (Barbados), Albert Padmore (Barbados), Viv Richards (Leeward Islands), Andy Roberts (Leeward Islands), Lawrence Rowe (Jamaica) and Elquemedo Willett (Leeward Islands). It was an excitingly experimental West Indian party and by no means all of us returned home with our reputations enhanced or even entact. One or two of those names have hardly been heard of since and took little further part in international cricket. For others, like Viv, Andy and myself, the tour became a springboard from which our Test careers took off.

India came as a terrible shock for those of us who had never been there before. There were so many people, all of them staring at us wherever we went as if we had come from another planet. I found this unnerving and a little frightening. For instance, it was impossible to go more than a few yards from the safety of the hotel without encountering a horde of beggars, thrusting out their skinny hands for a rupee or two. In my naivety and my enthusiasm to see everything possible, I left the hotel soon after arriving at Bombay and went for a walk. Never have I seen such poverty in the centre of a city and in the face of the beggars and the appalling stench, I retreated to the hotel for several days until I plucked up enough courage to venture out again. The strangeness and the unfamiliarity brought the team together much more quickly than it might have done if we had been touring somewhere we all knew.

A trip to the famous Taj Mahal was marred by having to step over two dead bodies and it was not uncommon to find other bodies on the steps of hotels around what is nevertheless a beautiful and delightful country. There were other, traditional, problems. Everyone suffered at some time or another from upset stomachs and there was never any drinking water, only soda water. All the food, no matter what is was, tasted of curry and it took some time to come to terms with the change in diet.

The matches themselves were fantastic affairs: colourful, exciting and hugely popular. Little stands were filled to overflowing and the noise as spectacular as anything the West Indies could produce. It was nice just to be part of it all, to soak up the atmosphere and to take it all in. It really did not matter, to begin with, whether I played or not and it was simply nice to be part of a tour. We were not paid much for the tour but the thought that such an experience was coming to me free was extremely pleasant. My career in India began in Poona against West Zone and I could hardly have made a better start. Viv scored a century but I made 66 in the first innings and 69 in the second. Since the match was used by our players largely as practice, inevitably it was drawn. I was pleased with my start and figured that reasonable results in the next two matches would see me as a serious contender for a place in the First Test. Roy Fredericks was certain of one opener's place and the other, on paper at least, rested between myself, Baichan and Rowe, though the latter was beginning to bat lower in the order. It was crucial then, to get runs at Indore where we were due to play the Combined Universities.

All three of the main contenders—Fredericks, Baichan and myself—were named in the team to play the universities and after dismissing them for 267, we built a huge reply of 546 for 4 against, it should be said, bowling which was something short of first class. The trouble was all three of us made runs and with 70 to my name, I was the one who came out of it worse. Fredericks made sure of his Test place with a sparkling 202 and Baichan, a thorough and solid little player, scored 158. The match was drawn but it hardly mattered. More important, it put me under some pressure to do well in our last pre-Test match, against South Zone at Hyderabad. Baichan was also in the side and he was 114 not out when we declared at 337 for one. My own contribution was 55 before I had to retire hurt with an injury which did not stop me scoring a brisk 32 in the second innings. Lawrence Rowe, the other possible contender, had run into trouble. After scoring 0 and 1 against West Zone, he complained of problems with his eyes. An optician in Poona was unable to diagnose the cause and Rowe struggled on to the last of the matches before the First Test. After scoring 15 not out against South Zone, his eyes were still causing him some worry. Opticians eventually told him that one eye was short-sighted and he flew to London immediately in a bid to get some specialist advice. There they told him not to go back to the tour and the decision was made not to replace him. With Rowe unfortunately out of the running, it seemed to rest between Baichan and I, both of us uncapped, for a vacant place in the Test team. When we reached Bangalore late in November for the start of the Test series, one of us was destined to lose out. It was him.

I was chosen to partner Fredericks in a side which also included Richards and Roberts. Our team was Greenidge, Fredericks, Kallicharran, Richards, Lloyd, Deryck Murray, Boyce, Barrett, Holder, Gibbs and Roberts. The team picked for Bangalore gave us plenty of batting, three pace bowlers in Roberts, Holder and Boyce and Gibbs, Barrett, Fredericks and Richards to share the spin attack. India chose their full complement of spinners in Chandra, Prasanna and Venkat to take advantage of the turning wickets India usually provides. As the day arrived, I was both nervous and excited at the prospect of making my Test debut but nerves took over completely when it was decided we should bat first. The atmosphere was incredible with India's supporters, a vast screaming army of people, adding to my fears as Fredericks and I walked out to bat. Just briefly my mind flashed back to the years of graft and torment, to the sheer hard work and even the tears. Here I was, aged 23, making my Test debut; I could hardly believe it. Reality seemed far away as I groped my way through the early deliveries from the medium-pace opening attack of Abid Ali and Solkar and my nerves almost accounted for me in the second over: I edged a ball firmly to second slip where the catch was grounded. Gradually I overcame my worries and soon settled down, once the spinners had started to operate, and the runs came comfortably and plentifully. Fredericks had to go off at one point and Alvin Kallicharran took his place. Alvin is one of the most technically correct batsmen I have ever played with and a punishing run scorer. Nothing the spinners could do with their various tricks induced the slightest problem and I had soon reached my 50. Still the runs came and in the heat of the Indian day, I began to think how easy it all was. If this was Test cricket then I ought to get a million runs.

Kallicharran and I had long since silenced the huge crowd and the score was standing at 177 with nothing seemingly between us and a colossal score. The Indian bowlers were performing economically enough but there was little penetration and at 93 a century in my first Test innings beckoned. It was then that disaster struck, a disaster entirely of our own making. Sunil Gavaskar was standing at short mid-on when I played a ball firmly to his left. I was positive the ball was going wide of him and called for a single. Kalli meanwhile was looking at the ball and had not heeded my call. Gavaskar had just got a hand to the ball to take a little of the pace from it and had run after it. Kalli was still glued to the spot, mesmerised by the activity, and seeing me half way down the wicket, screamed for me to get back. It was too late, Gavaskar had retrieved the ball and as I desperately tried to make my ground, the throw was too accurate and too quick. C. G. Greenidge run out 93. I was furious and as I trooped back dejectedly towards the pavilion I told Kalli he should have been paying attention. Kalli apologised, but the damage was done.

Kallicharran went on to make 124 but once they had broken through, the Indian spinners induced a collapse and we were all out for 289, a disappointing score in view of our earlier dominance. Holder and Roberts each took 3 wickets and India were dismissed for 260, making a good start to our second innings absolutely imperative. With Fredericks still not ready to open with me, Deryck Murray was promoted in the order as we sought to build on a slender lead. Murray was out without scoring and two more wickets fell by the time we had reached 75. I had started nervously again but the shots were coming without trouble and I was deter mined to make up for the previous disappointment with another big score.

Chandra was causing some concern with those almost freak deliveries of his, some of which come through at quicker than medium pace. One of his deliveries surprised Fredericks so much in the first innings that he twisted his ankle fending off a viciously spinning bouncer. In the second innings, he shocked me with a similar effort which rose up and hit me in the eye, but I soon felt confident enough to hit him for 2 sixes. In the first innings Chandra had provided me with a ball from which I hit my first Test six, a hooked shot which sailed over the boundary. Of all the sixes I have hit in my years as a cricketer, this is the one that lives longest in the memory and the one which I still regard as my best. This is not because it went the greatest distance or because I hit it harder than any previous six. It is merely because of what it represented: a big hit in my first Test. Once again, I reached 50 without being unruly troubled and the thought came to me that a century was here for the taking if I kept cool and avoided any incidents similar to the one a day or two beforehand. Clive Lloyd was my partner at the crease by now and his calming influence did much to smooth the way as runs came from both ends almost at will. Once more I found myself in the 90s. Surely nothing would go wrong this time? The nerves returned as never before and I grabbed each run like a man possessed. At last I passed the 100 mark to a massive sigh of relief from myself. I was out a few minutes later for 107 but the sense of achievement lived with me for days. Never in my wildest dreams had I expected to join a select band of players who had scored hundreds on their Test debut. But in the glow of self-satisfaction afterwards I could not help thinking back to that stupid run out which I now realised had stopped me making history. Clive surpassed my score by making 163 and, with two men injured, India were all out for 118 chasing 386. If this was Test cricket, I wanted more.

After the ease with which I adjusted to the demands of Test cricket, I made the fundamental mistake of thinking that I was now a world-class player capable of destroying any attack anywhere in the world. My over-confidence made the rest of the tour something of an anti-climax because, although I had my moments, I was never able to maintain the brilliance of my Test debut. I found myself making promising starts but then getting out to ridiculous shots which did me no credit. Against North Zone at Jullunder in a warm-up match for the Second Test, I scored 71 and 46 and felt there was nothing in the world to stop me repeating my success at Delhi where the Second Test was being played. I should have known better. With Roberts taking 3 wickets and the other bowlers sharing the rest, India were all out for 220 on a nice batting wicket. Here was a great chance for another big score against the gentle medium-pacers and a spin attack now reinforced by the great Bishen Bedi. Deryck Murray was my opening partner but he was out without scoring. Once more there was nothing to trouble me and I was quickly to 31 and playing with nerveless serenity when, in my complacency, I edged Prasanna to Engineer at the wicket. I was furious and my punishment was to sit in the pavilion and watch the rest of the side scoring the runs which could so easily have been mine. Viv Richards, making up for the single-figure disappointments at Bangalore, went on to make 192 and served notice on the cricketing public that a star was born. We were all out for 493 and won by an innings and 17 with as much ease as the result suggests. The Delhi victory put us 2–0 up with three to play. It seemed all over bar the shouting, which on Indian grounds is quite considerable. How wrong events proved us to be.

India was still proving a fascinating experience, almost daily throwing up something new for all of us. And nothing, either before or since, has quite matched the weirdest break I have ever known during a match. We were playing one of the Zone sides and fielding during another hot and sweaty day. As usual there was a

My worst moments: out for a 'pair' at Brisbane in the First Test in 1975.
(a) A ring of close Australian fielders get ready to appeal as a ball from Lillee
strikes me on the pads. Greenidge lbw bowled Lillee 0

(b) Gary Gilmour applauds
as I touch a ball to Rick
McCosker in the slips.
Greenidge c McCosker
b Gilmour 0

World Cup memento. Prince Philip has a smile and a medal for me after we had won the World Cup in 1975 (*Patrick Eagar*)

Celebration time. Clive Lloyd perches the 1975 Prudential World Cup on Alvin Kallicharran surrounded by (left to right) Gibbs, Kanhai, Greenidge, Deryck Murray, Holder, Roberts, Boyce, Richards and Julien

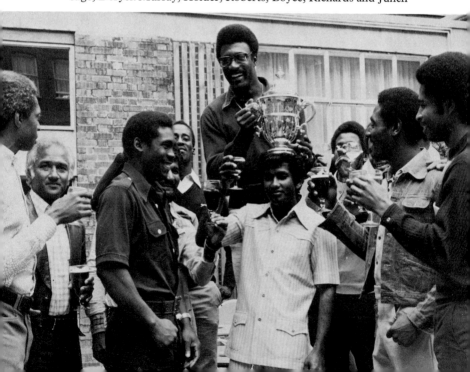

big and noisy crowd clamouring for runs, wickets and everything else. Suddenly they all went quiet as if someone had switched off a radio. We stood perplexed as large sections of them seemed to fall to the ground as if they had been killed. Then we noticed a strange black cloud moving at great speed in no apparent direction. This amazing sight was beginning to worry us when we heard the directions: *'Get down!'* With that command we all fell to the ground as a swarm of bees passed overhead with a deadly hum before disappearing as quickly as they had arrived. There were times too, when the exuberance of the volatile crowds got the better of them. I well remember Bernard Julien fielding down at third man near the boundary. Suddenly there were two loud bangs and before we knew what had happened Julien was running towards the wicket as if his life depended on it. Apparently the crowd had decided to surprise him as he dozed quietly in the outfield by throwing firecrackers at him. Of course, he just about jumped out of his skin as the firecrackers exploded around him and he decided discretion was the better part of valour and ran in to join the slip cordon for the sake of safety. I don't think Bernard ever got over the experience and every time he was subsequently asked to field down by the boundary he always came up with a plausible excuse not to. In India anything was possible and every stop on the itinerary produced its own minor dramas.

Another big provincial win, this time over Central Zone, set us up nicely for the Third Test at Calcutta, where we hoped to wrap up the series. India were getting a little desperate and brought back Chandra for Venkat and brought in a fresh new-ball bowling attack in Ghavri and Madan Lal. Andy Roberts continued his impressive series, hot on the heels of his successes for Hampshire the previous summer, and took 5 wickets for 50 on a wicket more helpful to the spinners. India were all out for 233 and once more I went out to bat more confident than I should have been. I had made 20 when Madan Lal had me caught. Fredericks, my partner, went on to make 100 but we only just scraped into a first innings lead, thanks to an error of judgement by Viv Richards. Viv had made 15 and looked set to emulate his big innings of the previous

Test when he was run out, scrambling to his crease on all fours, trying to get back from a non-existent single. Viv's wicket was crucial and with only a 7-run lead to defend, India scented we were not happy. Viswanath scored a fine century and we were left with a victory target of 310. The gentle medium-paced swing of Ghavri had me lbw for 3 and with only Kalli looking at ease, we were beaten by 85 runs. Looking back, I believe Viv's strange dismissal was the turning point. Had he survived and prospered as he threatened to do, then India's brief hopes would have faded and died. India's win gave them new heart and they went into the Fourth Test early in January full of justifiable hope. Madras was the setting and the first morning of the match provided a controversial happening at the centre of which was yours truly.

Farokh Engineer, the most prized Indian wicketkeeper and their most experienced batsman, had made 14 when he touched a ball from Julien to me at second slip. The ball came off the bat extremely fast and instinctively I grabbed at the ball at my ankles. It lodged between my fingers and I held it up in triumph. Everything happened so quickly and I was soon engulfed by my grateful team-mates but Engineer stood his ground momentarily believing the catch had not been clean. The umpire gave him out and his crucial wicket had been safely taken. I was not sure what the trouble was about, but next day when I picked up the papers I soon found out. There was a picture, prominently displayed, revealing that the catch had been grounded. It may sound strange, but anyone who has ever fielded at slip will know what I mean, when I say I was sure the catch was fair. If I had thought otherwise, I swear I would have admitted it and Engineer could have batted on. The picture shows that the ball hit the deck the very same moment it lodged between my fingers. No wonder Farokh waited for the signal and even now all I can do is apologise because at the time I had absolutely no idea it had been grounded. For all the gamesmanship in the game, I genuinely thought it to be a fair catch. Of course, next day when we went out to bat in reply to India's 190, there was a hail of boos and cat-calls to greet my walk to the wicket. I obliged them by making only 14 and if it had not been for Richards (50) we would have struggled to reach 192. Roberts took 5 Indian wickets in the second innings to give him match figures of 12 for 121 but the target of 255 always posed problems. Chandra's quicker ball bowled me for 17 and in spite of Kalli's 51, we were convincingly beaten by 100 runs. All of a sudden we were in danger of losing a series we had seemed destined to win with ease, and at 2–2 the Final Test at Bombay was of crucial importance.

When we first arrived in India we stayed in Bombay and saw their attempts to build a new stadium. With bamboo scaffolding and coconut palms for lining, the stadium was a long way from being ready. But when we arrived for the Fifth Test, a miracle had been performed. The mess of three months previously had been transformed and a fine new stand was ready to take in another massive number of spectators. The match was an intensively fought as you would expect from two teams on the threshold of winning the series. India brought back Solkar for Madan Lal and we had Arthur Barrett's spin in place of Keith Boyce. After nearly three months in India, we were determined not to settle for a draw. I imagine India were equally vehement about not letting us escape, having clawed their way back from 2–0 down.

The West Indies batted first and Roy Fredericks and I put on 81 unflustered runs before I was caught at the wicket, so providing Engineer with some measure of revenge. Disappointed I may have been, but Fredericks (104), Kallicharran (98), Murray (91) and a truly magnificent 242 not out from Clive Lloyd gave us an unassailable 604 for 6 before Lloyd declared. To their credit, India refused to let this huge total intimidate them and with big scores from Gavaskar, Viswanath, Gaekwad and a century from Solkar, they did well to reach 406. It meant we were forced to bat again and this time I was determined to end the series with a reasonable score. I was soon in my stride and had made 54 when Bedi removed me. Clive declared at 205 for 3 and the Indians were left with 404 to wind up an exciting series with a sensational win. But, in the chase for runs, they lost their first 6 wickets for 89 and were eventually all out for 202. My tour room-mate and friend, Van

Holder, claimed 6 wickets for 39 and a tough and rewarding rubber was ours.

There was time enough on the remainder of the Indian leg of our tour for me to inflict on myself an injury bad enough to make me a passenger for the rest of our Eastern trip. We were playing the last 45 minutes of the Final Test when Deryck Murray went off the field and I was thrust into his wicketkeeping job. For a novice, I did not do such a bad job. Then, in my enthusiasm, I made a spectacular dive to my left and hurt my back. I was carried back to the dressing room and was unable to move for half an hour. There was an excruciating pain in my leg and in my back and a hot shower provided only temporary relief. The stiffness returned and literally I seized up. I was taken to hospital for treatment with the pain worsening by the minute. If there is one place I hate, it's hospital. Just the smell of them is enough to make me run a mile, but running was the last thing of which I was capable at the time. The Indian doctors spoke to each other in a language of which I understood not a word before they explained to me in English that that they thought I had trapped a nerve. They gave me a cortisone injection and then laid me on a sort of couch. What was going to happen next? I soon found out, and it is no joke when I say it gave me quite a shock. What seemed like a million volts were pumping through my body and I took off from the table like something out of a Tom and Jerry cartoon. I almost had to be scraped off the ceiling and the pain was by now even worse. Eventually I was discharged, but the injury was a long time healing and I took little further part in the rest of the tour.

Three matches at Colombo against Sri Lanka provided welcome relief from the exertions of a five Test series in India and I was grateful to give my back some rest. We were in the beautiful island only for about two weeks and then it was time to move on to Pakistan. My injury showed no real sign of improving enough to allow me to start training and practising in earnest. I found it almost impossible to bend properly and the thought crossed my mind that I ought to return to England for expert treatment and diagnosis. Some light sessions in the nets did nothing to persuade me that I was ready for a comeback. So when the team was announced for the First Test in Lahore, I was ruled out immediately and Len Baichan got his chance at last. I was forced to sit in the stands as Roberts valiantly ran through the Pakistan first innings to take 5 for 66 and then Kallicharran helped us to a narrow lead with an unbeaten 92. Mushtaq scored a century and we were left with time enough to chase 359. This was Baichan's big moment and he batted through for 105 no out and at 258 for 4, we were able to hold out for a draw. This left me one match before the second and last Test in Karachi. It was against the Patron's XI at Rawalpindi and with scores of 27 and 13 not out, I felt I was not ready to return. It was with a sense of great regret that I was forced to sit out another Test match. In a high-scoring game, Julien and Kallicharran each made centuries and with Wasim Raja and Majid Khan doing likewise for Pakistan, a draw was a predictable and disappointing result. There were times during the lulls in play that I began to think the injury might even force me out of the game altogether, but it was definitely improving when we bade farewell at the end of an arduous but immensely enjoyable tour.

Maybe I had not lived up to the promise of that debut at Bangalore, but I felt I had done well enough to warrant a place in the World Cup which was to take place in England later in the summer. I thought I had done enough generally to have established myself in the West Indian team and in retrospect, I suppose it is as much as I could have expected. The West Indian team for the next few years was beginning to take shape and, with Richards and Roberts, I had made it clear that I was going to be one of the team's foundations. Not only had the tour set me up internationally, it had done something to raise my status in England and to lay the ghost of those comparative failures in Barbados. I got off the plane in England, four months older and wiser and as a rapidly emerging star. In five Tests in India I had come out with 371 runs at an average of 41. But, having done so well on the spinners' wickets of the East, I wrongly anticipated that Test cricket, on the whole, was quite easy stuff. I should have realised that the Indian bowling lacked any semblance of venom and been slightly more analytical about my success. In short, I thought I had got Test cricket worked out and I should have known better. The World Cup soon brought me back to earth and the following winter's failures in Australia positively destroyed my decreasing self-belief. I'm afraid I came back to England thinking I knew more than I did and the penalties for such cockiness are all the harder to bear. Having said all that, I will always look back on my first tour with affection and warmth. At no cost to myself I saw parts of the world I would not otherwise have seen and, for that at least, I shall be eternally grateful.

9 World Cup Worries

The first World Cup was obviously going to dominate the 1975 season and with our reputation for fast scoring the West Indies were made favourites even before we had named our fourteen-man squad. After my comparative success in India, I had expected to be in the squad and I was. We brought only one spinner in Lance Gibbs and from the party which performed in India, there was no Barrett, no Baichan, no Willett, no Padmore, no Rowe and no David Murray. Rohan Kanhai, a surprise to some, was recalled and two useful all-rounders were added to what was essentially a party for one-day matches. They were the Jamaican, Maurice Foster, and the young Barbadian Collis King, later to become a Glamorgan player and best man at my wedding. Our full squad was Lloyd, Deryck Murray, Boyce, Foster, Fredericks, Gibbs, Greenidge, Holder, Julien, Kallicharran, Kanhai, King, Richards, and Roberts. Our party assembled at the beginning of June for what was inevitably going to become a momentous occasion. The Australians had the Chappells, Lillee, Thomson and a fine team; England had played a lot of limited-over cricket individually and were playing on home territory, and Pakistan had enough brilliant strokemakers to beat any team in the world on their day. That, of course, is discounting teams like New Zealand and India who, according to the bookies, were merely there to make up the numbers. The event quickly captured the imagination of the public but it was not until we began to prepare in earnest for the competition that I realised just how seriously they were taking it. Everywhere we went, supporters of no particular team would come up and tell us of the gigantic sums of money passing over the counters of betting shops and in pubs and clubs. All of it on us to win. This

111

created its own pressures because we realised so much was expected of us. What's more, it soon became apparent that the sponsors were depending on the West Indies also to add spice to the event by playing in true 'calypso' style.

What everyone should have realised was that we were still a young and inexperienced team on the whole, with a couple of notable exceptions, and that few of us had ever encountered such concerted pressure from so many different sources. I believe this is one of the reasons why, personally, the Prudential World Cup of 1975 was not as great a success as it should have been. Only in the semi-final against New Zealand at the Oval did I get a half century and in the really important games, twice against the Aussies and once against Pakistan, I failed. I went into the World Cup with a curious mixture of apprehension at the unknown and over-confidence born of my winter in India. Because of India and because I knew all the English grounds so well, I had expected to be among the dominant characters of the new event. Our group, Group B, was the toughest. Only two could qualify for the semi-finals from ourselves, Pakistan, Australia and Sri Lanka, who were obviously not going to get very far in that sort of company. It amounted to two from three and if everyone of us played to our full capabilities then luck was going to play a deciding factor or sheer will-to-win. Sri Lanka provided us with little more than a gentle warm-up when we met them at Old Trafford in the first of our group matches. They were all out for 86 and we won by 9 wickets, thus reinforcing the optimism of the punters who had made us red-hot favourites. In the West Indies camp, we knew full well that we faced two really tough tests before we could start justifying this monetary faith. Pakistan was the next, formidable, hurdle to overcome and it was with some trepidation that we moved on to Edgbaston to meet them. They batted first in front of a crowd mixed equally between immigrants from Pakistan and from the West Indies, with a smattering of interested white faces among them. If they batted to their full capacity, we were in trouble.

Pakistan took advantage of a fine batting wicket and with nearly all their front-line batsmen scoring runs, a big total was inevitable.

Majid Khan made 60, Mushtaq 55 and Wasim Raja 58 as our bowlers toiled to stem the flow of runs. After 60 overs they had made 266 for 7, leaving a tremendous task, even by our standards, to earn us victory. I went out feeling both hesitant and nervous. So much was expected of me personally, I felt, and I was determined not to let anyone down. But I did. I managed only 4 and with other wickets falling cheaply, we were soon fighting a desperate battle for survival. Clive Lloyd rescued us briefly with 53, but he was out in controversial circumstances and returned to the pavilion a far-from-happy man. He slammed the door of the dressing room behind him in a fit of uncontrollable temper, threw his bat all around the room. The pressure on him as skipper was beginning to tell, and defeat and almost certain elimination were staring us in the face. At 203 for 9, defeat was little more than a formality. I was sitting glumly and silent, my bags packed for a quick exit. But the fall of the ninth wicket brought together Murray and Roberts for a historic last-wicket partnership and one of the most outstanding in limited-over cricket. Pakistan were rightly expecting to wrap up the match fairly promptly and Lloyd, still muttering to himself, had conceded victory. Gradually Murray and Roberts began to claw us back into the match. Each stolen single induced an increasingly visible amount of panic among the Pakistanis. Their hitherto impeccable fielding began to fall apart and the prospects of an unlikely win became more and more of a reality. The 250 came up but the overs were running out. The dressing room became a tense and exciting place to be. All of us shuffled around restlessly; one or two of the players refused to look. Each run was greeted with a rising crescendo of approval from our supporters.

Lloyd could hardly bear the tension. He sat in the corner demanding a commentary, an explanation for every ripple of crowd reaction. At last, with just two deliveries left, Murray (61 not out) saw us home to the most tremendous cheering I have ever encountered. As we all congratulated each other, as if we had won the cup itself, Lloyd raced from the dressing room out into the section of the pavilion stands reserved for members. 'That will teach

113

you . . . you cheats'! screamed poor Clive with a mixture of ecstatic relief and blind fury over his dismissal. Even in the hysteria of the moment, such behaviour did not go unnoticed and Clive was later severely reprimanded, I believe. Looking back, I think the Pakistan game, with its attendant emotion, was the turning point of the competition for us. We recovered our poise and the belief in ourselves and for me, it was the most memorable match of the whole competition—and that includes the final. Tom Graveney, the match adjudicator, gave the man-of-the-match award to the Pakistani bowler Sarfraz Nawaz whose 4 for 44 had threatened to win the match for his team. I am sure he would rather have not won the award and beaten us instead.

Since the Australians had already beaten them, Pakistan's challenge died with the Edgbaston defeat and so the clash between ourselves and the Aussies, scheduled four days later at the Oval, no longer quite had the edge of competition about it because we had both qualified for the semi-final. However it was in our interest to win because it would almost certainly ensure a comparatively easy semi-final against New Zealand. The losers would have to contend with England and their partisan crowd in the other semi-final. For all their ability and their toughness, the Australians were inexperienced when it came to the very different demands of limited-over cricket. It was armed with this knowledge that we made our way to the Oval, having just completed cricket's answer to the Great Escape.

At the Oval, Australia's lack of knowledge exposed itself with some panicky batting and they left us to get the manageable total of 192 in our alloted 60 overs. Ross Edwards scored 58 for Australia in the middle order and Rod Marsh was unbeaten with 52, but there was justifiable optimism in the West Indies dressing room at the prospect of chasing such a reasonable target. Roy Fredericks and I began the reply and for the first time I was up against the twin threat of Lillee and Thomson, the pair of fast bowlers who had made such a good job of demolishing England's veteran tourists only a few months previously. I felt quite confident and, having heard so much about these fast bowlers, was keen to have a

114

closer look. I had batted soundly enough for 16 before I became the first man out, but Fredericks (58) and Alvin Kallicharran (78) soon got s grip of the bowling to such an extent that we went on to win by 7 wickets with 14 overs to spare, which in one-day terms, is a thrashing of major proportions. Even then, the Australians were muttering about revenge, given the chance, but faced by England in the semi-finals, we did not give much for their hopes. England had finished top of their group and were to play Australia, while we had the comparatively easy task of playing New Zealand at the Oval.

The match against the New Zealanders was the one time in the entire series that I did proper justice to myself and produced the form, albeit momentarily, which I and the public had come to expect. As far as I was concerned, it was the one bright spot in a competition in which I was not as successful as I should have been. New Zealander had plenty of talent on show, but they expected to lose and could not have been surprised when they did. Only Geoff Howarth, as a Surrey player, operating on his home pitch offered any real resistance with 51 but the others succumbed to Bernard Julien.

It was about as much as New Zealand could do to muster 158 against Julien, who took 4 for 27, and the rest of our bowlers. Armed with little real retaliatory pace, the New Zealanders had no realistic hopes of winning and with as fluent a 55 as was possible in the circumstances, I led the way to a comprehensive victory. Kallicharran followed this up with 72 and in earning his second successive man-of-the-match award, saw us safely into the final with something like 19 overs to spare and 5 wickets still in hand. In the other semi-final many wickets fell quickly but decisive contributions from Gary Gilmour saw Australia through to the final to give them the chance of the revenge they had sought so eagerly.

In the three or four days leading up to the final at Lords, the tension mounted and the pressures increased. Every time we went to the nets to practise there were hordes of people to watch us, all seemingly ready to tell us how much was expected. All the neutrals were supporting us by now and the sports pages of the papers carried nothing else except the prospects for the big match. We posed for what appeared like hours for pictures and for the television cameras and radio microphones sprang up around us like mushrooms in a field. The papers were filled with bellicose quotes from the Aussies; of what Lillee, Thomson and the others were going to do to us and for the younger members of the squad, me included, the whole scene was frighteningly new and unnerving. Never before had I and many of the others come under so much pressure, none of it of our own making. The match had really caught the attention of the British cricketing public and it did not help my preparations to see eminent names within the game, writing that I held the key to the match. This sort of accolade, however well intended, only added to the immense strain we all felt in the three days before we headed for Lords, the home of cricket, and for many, the biggest day of our lives.

Lords was in festive mood for the occasion. All the pre-match publicity about this, the first Prudential World Cup Final, had given the day an edge which as a player is almost impossible to describe. Every seat had been sold, every nook and cranny of this ancient ground bulged with people, noise and expectation. What seemed like thousands were there early just to greet our arrival and with a vast army of our own supporters crammed inside to witness this momentous day, the players were filled with trepidation. The pressure made the Australians fill with the sort of determination which is their national characteristic. Most of our players responded positively also and the match was as memorable as the occasion deserved. For my own part, I was as nervous as at any time in my career. I wanted to do well on such a big and important day but the apprehension and the pressures of the previous three days and the whole competition were possibly beginning to get the better of me at a time when I needed my wits and composure most. We were to bat first in the most fantastic atmosphere I had known for a cricket match and I remember, as I put my pads on, the cold beads of sweat running down my cheeks and the quivering hand on the straps. The hum of the crowd broke into a roar as the Australians

116

came out from the cool of the pavilion, down the steps and on to the immaculate turf of Lords. The time came for Fredericks and me to make our way out to do battle as the sun rose high for another perfect summer's day. Doors were opened for us, cries from well-wishers filled the air as we walked out into the sun; the West Indians among the crowd broke into hysterical cheering. Walking out to bat that day is now but a blur on the memory. The sheer nervousness gave me a sort of floating sensation and my only thought was to get it all behind me and get some action under my belt.

Lillee, Thomson and the rest were soon firing away as if this too was the most important match of their lives and my usual aggression was tempered by the need to see the shine off the new ball. It was imperative for us to make a solid start because, with so many strokemakers still to come, there was no need for us to take undue risks so early in the day. There was an incredible sort of buzzing noise about this huge crowd between the action but every time a ball was bowled the West Indian section burst into a cacophony of either approval or dismay, depending on what had happened to that particular delivery. We had done well to take the score to 12 when the first major incident set the match alight. Fredericks hooked a Lillee bouncer for six, but as the crowd rose as one to salute a magnificent shot, Fredericks was already making his way back to the pavilion. He had trodden on his wicket while executing the shot and we had lost a vital batsman. Kallicharran, for whom the competition had been a great personal success, was soon in his stride but a catch behind the wicket off Gilmour made us 27 for 2 and the overs fast disappearing. The harder I tried to push the score along, the worse it became. All my best shots were cut off and there was enough playing and missing from me to encourage the bowlers into the belief that I may not be staying long. At last we reached 50 and I was still there but the West Indian cheers did not last long. Thomson, whom I do not rate as highly as Lillee, induced me to edge a ball just outside the off-stump to wicket-keeper Marsh and I was out for 13. Walking back to the pavilion I was having mixed feelings, while my dismissal was being analysed over and over again by slow-motion on television. At 50 for 3 there was scarcely room for congratulations, and after many overs of struggle 13 was by no means a big reward. But the edge of the fast bowling had been taken off and the way was open for Kanhai, Lloyd and the others to reap the benefits of our earlier vigil.

This was Clive's match, though, and, with the confidence of a man who knew his moment had arrived, he began a punishing assault on the Australians. With the experienced Kanhai as his watchful partner, Lloyd played the major role in a partnership for the fourth wicket of 149. It was the crucial stand of the match and the Australians, after their promising start, all but wilted under Clive's aggression. Kanhai was out eventually for 55 and Viv Richards, more nervous than now seems possible, betrayed his feelings when out soon afterwards. After a tremendous barrage of shots, Clive was caught at the wicket soon after completing a memorable century. Once more the Aussies glimpsed a chance with the West Indies 209 for 6, but Keith Boyce and Bernard Julien—good men to have at numbers seven and eight—restored our advantage and there were enough runs from the tail to give us 291 for 8, leaving the Australians something like 5 an over to beat us. The mood in the dressing room was now decidedly buoyant. With Roberts, Julien, Boyce, Holder and Lloyd himself to share the bowling, we had good reason to expect the Australians to find runs hard to come by. McCosker's early dismissal reinforced our optimism but once Ian Chappell arrived at the crease a major obstacle appeared in our path to the cup. Ian is a desperately difficult man to remove and the situation could not have been better tailor-made for him when he came in with the score at 25 for 1. With Alan Turner's solid support, the score moved on to 81 before we had our next success. Turner became the first of five men run out in the Australian innings, once more betraying their inexperience of this type of cricket and letting us recover when perhaps we might not have done.

Viv Richards ran out two of their batsmen who could not work out the difference between haste and panic and with both Chappells out that way, Ian for 62 and Greg for 15, we were entitled to think the game was ours. But, as we were to learn the hard way a few months later, the Australians are never beaten until the last man is out and slowly they fought their way back into a match which we were wrong in assuming was ours already. Rod Marsh, Doug Walters with a fine 35, and Ross Edwards (28) started to tilt the balance back in their direction and I remember Clive beginning to have increasingly urgent conferences with his lieutenant, Deryck Murray. Apart from the suicidal run-outs, only Keith Boyce was taking wickets and on a perfect batting surface none of our strike bowlers was achieving anything like a breakthrough. With the summer shadows beginning to lengthen and the overs slowly passing, the crowd became more hysterical by the minute as Australia passed 200 with only 6 men out. Then came a little collapse and at 233 for 9, our supporters, who had hitherto needed little excuse for running out to the middle, were in jubilant mood. Banners were being waved from all corners of the ground and the drums and beer cans filled with pebbles made a deafening victory crescendo. How premature they were. Lillee and Thomson came together as accomplished batsmen and in chaotic circumstances with crowds on the pitch, they inched their way nearer our total. There is no denying now that we were showing every sign of losing the match. Field placing was becoming ragged and the bowling sloppier and less accurate than at any time during the day. Eight balls left and only 18 were needed for the Australians to clinch what would have been a sensational win by any standards. It was then that Thomson was carelessly run out and the cup was ours at last. What scenes at the moment of our triumph. Ecstatic West Indian supporters were everywhere and it was some back-bruising time later before Clive Lloyd, the man of the match, held the cup aloft. A truly incredible day, but much as I enjoyed it, I was glad when it was all over.

After the World Cup interlude, returning to the mundanities of county life was both an anti-climax and a welcome relief. As a cricketer, and maybe as a person as well, I grew up a lot in the few short weeks of the World Cup's progress. I learned that after my success in India I still had a long way to go before I could truly say

I was a world-class batsman. I also believe that while we beat the Australians in such euphoric circumstances, they gained an important psychological advantage by showing us that they were not going to be intimidated by our greater talent and making it abundantly clear that the West Indies tour of Australia later in the year would be an entirely different encounter.

Returning to county cricket, I discovered that Hampshire were still an important force. We finished the season in third place eventually to add to the first and second placings of the previous seasons. Yorkshire, the runners-up, ended with only one point more but there was no disputing Leicestershire's right to the championship—16 points clear of the field. We made up for this by winning the John Player League for the first time in Hampshire's history and so adding another important medal to my collection. After the World Cup winners' memento in the same season, I could hardly have asked for more. It was also the season, though, in which I played two of the most memorable innings of my career so that 1975 was very much a landmark. We were still in with a chance of winning the county championship when I scored what to date is the highest total by a Hampshire batsman since the war. Defeats notably by Glamorgan and Middlesex had set us back but we went into the match against Sussex at Southampton only two points behind the leaders, Yorkshire with a game in hand and only three to play. Needless to say, the ground was packed again and expectation high. We really felt we could make up for the disappointments of the previous summer by winning the title emphatically this time.

Sussex were terribly weak that day. They were without John Snow, Greig, Buss and everyone else who mattered and I have no wish to be modest falsely when I say that scoring 259 against their attack was no great achievement. It only took me little over five hours but it was all so easy. They had no bowlers of anything more than medium pace and on a blisteringly hot day, those that did bowl soon got tired. I hit 13 sixes, a championship record, but I am hard pushed to remember any more than one of them which broke a window in the flats overlooking the ground, thereby achieving a

The West Indian team party for 1975–76 in Australia with team managers. The players are (left to right, back row): Greenidge, Julien, Holding, Holder, Lloyd, Padmore, Roberts, Boyce, Gibbs. Front row: Baichan, David Murray, Inshan Ali, Kallicharran, Deryck Murray, Rowe, Richards and Fredericks

Mrs Grace Mendoza, aged 67, meets the man who did all the damage. Mrs Mendoza was hit on the knee by a shot from me during the Lord's Test in 1976 and required treatment. Later she asked to meet me to talk about the incident

career-long ambition. Every time I reached a 50, it was signalled by a six and since then I am often asked if this was deliberate. The answer to that is, it certainly was not. At one stage I lost track of my runs and so every six was merely a coincidence. I did not realise I had done it at every half century until Gilliat, my partner for the fourth wicket, told me about it. I can assure you, it came as a pleasant surprise and I promptly hit another one to bring up my 200. I only wish after all that, I could turn round and say how much I enjoyed this massacre. I do not wish to sound ungracious when I say that it all means little to me today. It was an annihilation and as such I did not enjoy it very much. For the sake of variety, I was standing outside the leg stump, willing the bowlers to bowl at the wide open stumps and then hitting the ball from outside leg stump over extra cover to the boundary. I enjoyed that shot more than any of my sixes (apart from the broken window) and having succeeded once, tried it again and again. This of course demoralised the Sussex attack to such an extent that after 100 overs we had amassed 501 for 5 and there seemed little our opponents could do except pray for rain. But on the same evening, Andy Roberts took his practice run-up, checked and then hobbled off the field and out of cricket for the rest of the season—just when we needed him most.

Without Roberts we still managed to contain Sussex well enough for them to have to follow on but we could not get them out a second time and we used ten bowlers, including the wicketkeeper, in a bid to dislodge them. I took three second innings wickets but the match degenerated into farce when the number nine batsman John Spencer was allowed to score 79 in what almost became the fastest century of the season. Sussex were all out for 524 and the chance of vital points slipped from our grasp. Much the same happened in our next match, against Derbyshire at Southampton. We built a big lead and then failed to get them out a second time. John Ward, a teacher who had never scored more than 37 and who had already been told he would not be needed next season, made 104 for Derbyshire and in collecting only eight bonus points, our challenge ground to a halt. As far as statistics are concerned, 1975

121

was a better year for me and in first-class matches for Hampshire 1,120 runs at an average of 41 was more what I had come to expect of myself.

In the cup competitions, Hampshire again failed when we looked the side best equipped to win at least one of them. The Gillette Cup did provide me with my other personal moment of glory in the season. We were playing Glamorgan at Southampton and Barry Richards and I enjoyed one of our greatest days, putting on 210 for the first wicket. Barry was first out for 129 but I carried on to make a Gillette Cup record of 177 which included 7 sixes and 17 fours. That was the day Malcolm Nash produced his white handkerchief in mock surrender and with figures of 2 for 84 from his 12 overs it might have been advisable for him to have done just that. Nash, with his left-arm swing, is an awkward customer in conditions favouring him and I am sure he has got the better of me on a number of occasions over the years. Having murdered Glamorgan, we were ourselves heavily beaten in the next round by Lancashire.

We came much closer to a Lords final in the Benson and Hedges Cup, but defeat at Leicester in the semi-final came as a bitter blow in a match we should have won. I scored 111 but our target of 217 was never enough and Leicestershire's solid discipline saw them beat us in the last over. If we failed in the cup competitions, we made up for our disappointments by winning the John Player League by two points from Worcestershire. I suppose my biggest contribution was a century against Somerset but I shall never forget the day we disappeared into the Derbyshire Dales and came out with the trophy. The match was to be played at the village ground of Darley Dale and we needed to win it to make sure of winning the title. I remember driving up and down a main road looking for the turn-off to Darley Dale and then registering some shock when at last we found it. There was a tiny pavilion and facilities which can hardly be described as first class. Tom Mottram kept up our spirits with his laconic humour but first inspections of the wicket did nothing to dispel fears that we could lose the title on a mudheap. The wicket was right in the middle of a field which looked as if it was used by cows for the rest of the year and heavy rain had made it slushy at one end. Luckily the boundaries were short because the grass held up even some of my shots to such an extent that certain fours were stopping dead about 10 yards from the bat. The match was being televised which caused problems for the BBC, but Barry and I made light of the problems by getting Hampshire off to a good start. I made 55 and my greatest moment of a memorable day was hitting the fast bowler, Alan Ward, over extra cover for six. I enjoyed it so much that I did it again. Derbyshire were simply not equipped to get 222 and we won by 70 runs. The champagne flowed that night in Darley Dale, a curious place to round off an eventful summer.

There was one other surprise bonus to the 1975 season for me. I won the national prize for the most sixes and although I have won similar prizes since, this one gave me a big fillip. I suppose the Sussex match and the 13 sixes helped clinch it, but an award like this out of all the players in the country is something I treasure and do so every time I win it. It shows that if there is one thing which I do more consistently than any other player in county cricket, it is hitting sixes. I suppose it is for sixes that I shall always be remembered, and there are worse ways to stay in the memory. It had been an exciting summer for me and with the tour to Australia less than two months away, there was much to look forward to. I expected to be in the party for the tour after the way things had gone and there's no doubt the West Indies were expecting big things from me in Australia. I was determined not to let them down and, after the way things had gone, there was no reason to suppose the winter of 1975–6 was not going to be equally successful. How wrong I was.

10 Australian Disaster

I doubt whether any series since the war had aroused as much speculation and eager anticipation as the West Indian tour to Australia in 1975–6. The Australians, still smarting from their World Cup defeat, believed their side as strong and well balanced as any in the last twenty years and the prospect of a six-Test series against the 'World Champions' had them drooling long before our seventeen-man squad headed south late in October. The Chappell brothers were at their peak and so too were Lillee, Thomson and the underrated Max Walker. They might have lost Ross Edwards but Ian Redpath, as solid and dependable an opener as any, was more than adequate compensation for his absence and, as we were to discover, the key man to the whole battle. Our tour party was captained by Clive Lloyd and with Deryck Murray as his deputy, it had the look of a powerful combination, strong in all departments and boosted by the emergence of 'our secret weapon', a 21-year-old fast bowler from Jamaica, Michael Holding. What we lacked was not talent but experience and few of the players, writers or spectators who witnessed the tour ever made it clear properly that we were essentially a young side of whom only Lance Gibbs, Roy Fredericks and Lloyd himself had ever been to Australia. The rest had mostly only a couple of years Test cricket under our belts and our lack of experience was, of course, ruthlessly exposed. I am already making excuses for what was a collective debacle and a personal nightmare so painful that I have spent my life since trying to erase it from my memory. For the record, we lost the Test series 5–1 and from my point of view it was the biggest setback of my life—a veritable disaster.

The West Indian party was Clive Lloyd (Guyana, captain), Deryck Murray (Trinidad, vice-captain), Len Baichan (Guyana), Keith Boyce (Barbados), Roy Fredericks (Guyana), Lance Gibbs

(Guyana), Gordon Greenidge (Barbados), Vanburn Holder (Barbados), Mike Holding (Jamaica), Inshan Ali (Trinidad), Bernard Julien (Trinidad), Alvin Kallicharran (Guyana), David Murray (Barbados), Albert Padmore (Barbados), Viv Richards (Combined Islands), Andy Roberts (Combined Islands) and Lawrence Rowe (Jamaica). The West Indian selectors had good reason to believe that this group of players could return from Australia having beaten them on their own soil for the first time. There were Roberts and Holding to provide the new-ball attack, with Holder, Boyce and Julien a strong trio to augment their pace. Padmore and Inshan Ali were cover for the spin of the veteran Gibbs and there was enough class batting to survive injuries, loss of form and anything the hostile Aussies could bounce at us. So much for theory. Instead, we limped home defeated, dispirited and our morale in tatters. My own reputation had suffered more than most as 11 runs in four Test innings will testify, but my confidence had been badly shattered and on the plane home there were moments when I thought of packing it all in. Awful as it is, I shall search my memory and recall the events of the four unhappiest months of my life and tell my version of why it all went wrong; of why we singularly failed to use our ability and why 'The Greatest Series' was reduced to little more than a farce.

Two one-day matches in the lovely surroundings of Papua-New Guinea set us up nicely for Australia. The players enjoyed the stop and it gave us a chance to renew old acquaintances among the tour party. The managers, Esmond Kentish and Keith Walcott and Lloyd, told us it was going to be tough but there was not a player among us not looking forward to taking on the Aussies on their own wickets. It was the ultimate test for many of us.

Nothing could have been more breath-taking than Australia when we first arrived in that vast country. The Australians could not have been more friendly. They welcomed us with open arms and we were feted as special guests wherever we went in those first few days. There was the visit to the races to see the prestigious Melbourne Cup and there was champagne from the backs of Rolls-Royces. Five cars (not Rolls-Royces) were put at the disposal of the

125

team at every port of call and nothing was too good for us at the hotels. We were wined and dined and honoured at every available opportunity. With the sun shining, we all thought we had come to paradise. I came to love the trees and spires of Adelaide almost immediately and blood-curdling confrontation seemed a million miles away. In short, I thought I had come to a tremendous country and I could hardly wait for the action to begin.

The first hints of what was to come, overtook us at Adelaide after a couple of leisurely warm-up matches. We ran into a 6 foot 7 inches fast bowler, Wayne Prior, playing for South Australia. Prior was an ex-gravedigger and a good enough prospect to be signed later by Kerry Packer. However, he greeted us with a hail of bumpers and the sort of language to make a trooper blush. Every ball which beat the bat either brought an appeal or a string of expletives informing us how lucky we had been to survive that particular delivery. Gary Cosier scored a century for South Australia but the match was drawn and we moved on to Victoria a little taken-aback by the win-at-all-costs attitude of our first serious opponents.

It was in Melbourne at the colossal and rambling concrete stadium of the MCG that we ran into Ian Redpath for the first time. Redpath, nearing the end of his career, was new to us because he had not been in England for 1975, but his Test record marked him out as a man who could provide a considerable obstacle if he was to regain his place in the national side. Redpath was Australia's answer to Geoff Boycott, content to occupy the crease for motionless hour after hour and to accumulate runs rather than score them. Nothing worried him, least of all the fast bowlers and he blunted our pace attack on more than one crucial occasion. 'Redders', a wirily built antique dealer, scored 105 in Victoria's first innings and in so doing, scored an important psychological victory over the West Indian bowlers. Later he was to go on and make three Test centuries against us and to end up with an aggregate of something like 600 runs in that customarily gritty manner of his. Nothing Roberts, Holding or any of the others could do disturbed his concentration or his calm control and for my money, he was the man of the entire series. At one stage we thought of trying to unnerve him with a concerted campaign of bouncers but Redpath never flinched and he amazed us by pawing down some of these bouncers with his hand, like a man swatting a troublesome fly. I cannot remember ever seeing a batsman doing anything similar either before or since and you have to remember that he was doing it on fast wickets to deliveries hurled down by people of the pace of Roberts and Holding. It makes me shudder at his bravery, but he destroyed our attack by his obduracy and with every hour he spent at the wicket, our morale slumped further and further.

Alan Hurst took 7 wickets to confirm our fear that there was a plentiful supply of quick bowlers in Australia but I made 61 in our only innings of a drawn match and left Melbourne pretty pleased with my start. I followed this by making 93 against Western New South Wales at Dubbo and there was nothing to suggest the traumas to come. It was against New South Wales at the Sydney Cricket Ground that I ran into trouble for the first time, literally. My scores of 8 and 35 were barely satisfactory but the real damage was done when fielding. I was chasing a ball towards the boundary when my hand became caught on the picket fence. The injury needed some hospital attention but although it was nothing serious, two of my fingers needed covering for many months afterwards. I am not using that as an excuse for subsequent failures but the knowledge that my right hand was not as good as it should be nagged at the back of my mind for the rest of the tour and affected my approach to both batting and fielding. Mike Holding, who had already scored two half centuries, took 6 wickets in the New South Wales second innings and we won convincingly. The extra bounce and pace in the wicket, plus the readily available supply of fast bowlers to exploit them, caused me the same sort of worry as when I first arrived in Barbados from the softer English conditions.

There was still nothing to disturb the steady build-up for the first Test at Brisbane and we had the chance to get to know the 'Gabba by playing Greg Chappell's Queensland a few days before the scheduled start. Brisbane has a fine, new stadium, probably as modern as any in the world and Inshan Ali's left-arm spin enabled

127

us to win by an innings. We could not have been in better heart for the start of the Test series five days later on an adjoining wicket.

My hand was not bad enough to force me to miss the match and we were able to field a full-strength side with Inshan Ali's success against Queensland earning him a chance to do the same against Australia. Lillee and Thomson had been saying some bellicose things in the papers and on television but the Australians, too, thought the pitch might take spin because Terry Jenner came in for Max Walker. Like the rest of the team I was keenly anticipating this first major clash and having endured the tumultuous build-up to the World Cup final, the hysterical pro-Australian campaign in their press did little to unnerve us. There was a predictably big crowd at the 'Gabba for the first day and I was confident and well-prepared when Lloyd won the toss and chose to bat on a wicket which had caused some concern in the days leading up to the match. It was then that I encountered Lillee's tremendous charisma and his equally fierce determination again, having almost forgotten how tough a competitor he can be. Fredericks had taken the score to 3, but with the crowd baying for blood and wickets, I was not having a happy time. I played and missed at two deliveries from Lillee and the groans from the crowd and from the Australian players started to play on my nerves. I was beginning to think I would never get off the mark when I made one mistake too many and paid the penalty with my wicket. I thought a ball from Lillee was going well outside the off stump so, in the split second available to me, decided to raise my bat and pad-up. There was a horrendous cry from the ring of close fielders, the whole ground seemed to erupt and with Lillee roaring an appeal, I was given out leg before wicket. It was a basic error of technique and there was no real excuse. Not unnaturally, my team-mates were by no means sympathetic.

We never really recovered and only Deryck Murray's brave 66 enabled us to reach 214. The wicket was playing well by now, and Greg Chappell, like the supreme batsman he is, made 123 on it and with the left-hander, Alan Turner, scoring 81 we were in trouble, trailing by 152 on the first innings. It was with the shadows lengthening across the 'Gabba that Fredericks and I stepped out at the end of second day with a huge responsibility facing us. There was little chance of the West Indies winning the match—in fact none at all. Our only hope was to bat for as long as possible in the hope of atoning for our blunders in the first innings and holding out for a draw. I have to admit that I was in a state of near panic when we went out again; not just nervous but genuinely fearful of what might happen. Never in seven years of top cricket had I ever got a 'pair', two noughts in the same match. But as we made our way to the crease, the prospect of doing so preoccupied me. Fredericks was less nervous as you would expect of a man of his experience and it half occurred to me as we walked silently from the dressing room to ask him to help me get off the mark.

The Australians had their tails up with such a convincing lead and Lillee was getting ready to capitalise on it. My one and only ambition was to see out the day; to survive until tomorrow and the chance to take on such a good attack when fresh and ready. I was so nervous that I could feel the bat shaking in my hand as Lillee and Gilmour began to bowl at us. One or two deliveries I allowed to pass outside the off-stump and I was content to let Fredericks face as much of the bowling as possible. It was getting to the end of the day and the end of my ordeal when Fredericks was facing the last ball of the penultimate over—or so I thought.

Fredericks was batting quite confidently when, on the last ball of the over, he aimed to straight drive but mistimed it slightly and it flew along the ground towards wide mid-on. It had beaten the fielder and there was enough pace on the ball to get at least 3 runs. I was desperate to get away from the prospect of facing a whole over, but Fredericks was not even looking at the ball. He was so furious about not hitting it properly that he had turned from the action and was studying his bat. As a result, there was not even a single from a ball which could have brought us 3 and it left me in the firing line to see out an eight-ball over when I would rather have been anywhere else in the world. There was no escaping it. Gilmour bowled and with four slips and two gullies, there was proof that the Australians were anticipating a wicket and my trembling at the crease can only have acted as a spur. Three deliveries from Gilmour were safely negotiated and there were only five more to come. His left-arm action slanted the ball across me and away towards the slips. I was determined to avoid any risks but the fourth ball bounced higher than I had expected and I nudged at it. I tried to draw my bat away from it, but it was too late and the ball looped up off my glove to give fourth slip the gentlest of catches. Once more the crowd took off in sheer delight and McCosker and Gilmour, the principals in my dismissal, were engulfed by grateful team-mates. I was furious and heart-broken all at the same time. My worst fears about the dreaded 'pair' had been realised and, in my anguish and despair, I let Fredericks know what I thought about his stupid failure to take advantage of those 3 runs and to get me out of trouble. I am the first to acknowledge that I really have no one to blame but myself but I felt Fredericks might have spotted my ill-ease and done something to protect me. I have never forgiven him for that little incident and his refusal to accept any of the blame made it all the worse to bear.

I have no hesitation in saying this was the worst moment of my cricketing life and the unfortunate prelude to the rest of a disastrous tour. I was left with three days, the rest of the match, to mull over my failures. Rowe and Kallicharran each scored centuries and Murray made Australia sweat a bit while making 55. But even a total of 370 was not enough to provide anything other than temporary respite and, faced with a target of 219, the Aussies were far too professional to let us get away with it. McCosker and Turner were soon out but the Chappells came together and lingering hopes of a surprise win died with their growing command. Greg made his second century of the match and with Ian 74 not out, Australia were significantly ahead in the battle, having beaten us by 8 wickets with more than a day to spare. We headed 3,000 miles west to Perth with our morale badly hit by the setback and no one more dispirited than me.

I had expected a reproach from the management, a lecture or at best, some badly needed advice, but there was nothing. Not even a sympathetic 'bad lack' or any kind of inquest on my failures.

Neither of the managers nor Lloyd came forward to help me get over the catastrophes of Brisbane and to prepare me for the second Test. Holder and Rowe, as team-mates, told me not to let it get me down but the absence of comment from the tour leaders only contributed to my growing depression. Perhaps they resolved to say nothing deliberately and to let me sort it out for myself in the state match against Western Australia, which was the last chance before the next Test. Perth is the fastest wicket in Australia and probably the fastest in the world. Dennis Lillee grew up on it as did another great Australian bowler, Graham McKenzie and the need to do well there was important not just to me but to the West Indies as well. We had to equalise.

Western Australia always seem to perform well against touring sides and there was no exception when we met them at the WACA. I was glad at another chance to get some runs, but my scores of 3 and 29 did nothing for my confidence nor for other people's confidence in me. They beat us by 115 runs in a high-scoring match and I realised that if I was to get into the team for the Second Test it would be on reputation alone. On the other hand, I figured that I had never really let down the West Indies and my failures at Brisbane were my first in half-a-dozen Tests and the World Cup. As I saw it, the team selectors could leave me out and bring in either Baichan or Rowe, both of whom had considerable experience as openers. Imagine then how appalled I was when the team was announced. I had been dropped, which I had half expected, but the name of my replacement sent me into a state of shock. Bernard Julien was nominated as the man to take over as Fredericks opening partner. Now, I have nothing against Bernard. As a bowler and as a number seven, eight or nine batsman he is an extremely effective player. Yet he was being asked here to face Lillee, Thomson, Walker and Gilmour as an opener on the fastest wicket in the world. I drifted around for hours afterwards trying to get over the sensation. No one had taken the trouble to tell me why I was out and I became inconsolable. The whole thing was humiliating. Julien, to my knowledge, had never opened an innings before and now he was being asked to face some of the best bowlers in the

131

game while they were fresh and armed with the new ball.

Australia chose to bat first and despite 156 from Ian Chappell, we were pleased to get them all out for 329. Julien made 25 as a makeshift opener and I have to concede that he did not do a bad job, but an innings described by some veteran pundits as one of the greatest in Test match cricket swung the match our way. It came from Fredericks who made 169 in just over three and a half hours. With Lloyd making 149, we ended up with a big first-innings lead of 256.

As 12th man I was left to sit in the dressing room, morosely pondering my fate, but even as 12th man I soon ran into trouble. Australia were about to start their second innings just before tea and I had forgotten that Kallicharran was unable to field because his nose had been broken by a delivery from Lillee. I was not properly changed and ready when Lloyd led our players out to begin fielding and Inshan Ali, the 13th man, was hastily summoned to action while I completed my dressing. Inshan is not the best of fielders and while I got myself prepared the inevitable happened. Turner was soon out but immediately afterwards Ian Chappell, that most prized of wickets, skied a catch in Inshan's direction. The whole place held its breath as Inshan got underneath it and put it down. Ian did not last much longer, but when at last I came out and the humiliated Inshan departed, I was given the biggest roasting of my life. One by one they screamed abuse at me for not being there to hold the catch and it continued when we went inside for tea. I was given hell by everyone and although I apologised for not being ready, I had to ask them as my only defence why they were so sure that I would have held that particular catch anyway. But they insisted it was all my fault and, as the scapegoat, I was left to go away and sulk.

Next day Andy Roberts ran through them, taking 7 wickets for 54 and we had won the match by an innings and 87. There was jubilation in the camp because it was a match we had to win, and having won it so decisively, there was enough optimism among us to believe that we could go on and clinch the series. For my own part, there were two matches in which to regain my Test place. I dared not fail. The first was a one-day international at Adelaide. I made 41 but we lost, and against South Australia, scores of 3 and 64 must have shown the selectors that I was not yet a spent force.

This brought us to Melbourne and the Third Test at the giant MCG starting on Boxing Day. I could not believe that the selectors would change the side after it had massacred the Australians at Perth, so I was resigned to being left out again, in spite of my comparative success at Adelaide. We had a team meeting on Christmas Day soon after having lunch. Lloyd indicated that I was back in the team and that Keith Boyce was the man most likely to step down. I could have cried with laughter. Why was I back in? I had really done nothing to deserve a recall, just as I felt I had not been playing badly enough in the first place to be dropped. I was amazed by the team selections.

It was at this same meeting that Lance Gibbs, our senior professional and a venerable man, gave us some advice. The umpires were causing us some trouble with their poor decisions around the country and we had long since lost confidence in their impartiality. Gibbs, with some twenty-five years of cricket around the world behind him, conceded they were the worst in his memory, but told us to be adult about it and not let the decisions throw us out of our stride. His words seemed judicious and timely and we agreed to ignore the bad breaks from umpires and to get on with the game because, by now, we knew we were the better side. A matter of hours later Gibbs was bowling to Gary Cosier, making his Test debut in front of his home-city crowd. Cosier had barely opened his account when Gibbs beat him on the backfoot and rapped him on the pads. Gibbs screamed an appeal. Not out, said the umpire. Gibbs went beserk, snatched his cap from the umpire and bellowed: 'You cheat! This man is out!' The umpire should have reprimanded him but probably because Gibbs has a reputation for being easy-going and affable, ignored him. It was typical of the way decisions were going and Cosier went on to score a century.

For me, it was another disaster. Australia won the toss and put us in. The MCG filled with 85,000 people is an awesome sight and

Lillee and Thomson are their heroes. Try and imagine what it is like then, to mark your crease and see Lillee coming in at you, his teeth clenched and pendants swinging hypnotically around his neck. And all the time, a growing chant of 'Kill, kill' as he approaches the wicket. I can assure you, it is not a pleasant experience, if like me, you are on the receiving end. What is more, every time I played and missed there was not only the roar of the crowd to ridicule my efforts. There was the slip cordon to tell me in no uncertain terms that I had not been good enough to touch it. Such places are not for the faint-hearted and I had made only 3 when I edged Thomson to Marsh. Fredericks scored 59 but there were a succession of batting failures against Lillee and Thomson, who took 9 wickets between them, and we were all out for 224. Redpath then punished us with a dour century and with Cosier escaping to crown his debut with another ton, we wilted under the combined pressure of our own folly and the poor umpiring decisions. Australia's total of 485 gave them a colossal lead and for the second time on the tour, I was going out to bat again with the prospect of defeat staring at us. One well-struck four through mid-off lifted me slightly but after making 8, I edged Walker to Marsh again and retreated to the pavilion under a cloud of depression while thousands of beer-soaked Australians celebrated my demise. Lloyd scored a breathtaking 102 but our total of 312 left them only 52 to win and they made no mistake. It was a crushing defeat for us and, after doing so well to equalise at Perth, we knew it would take a monumental effort to come back a second time. The Aussies had got us on the run, and we knew it.

The Fourth Test at Sydney followed a matter of days later and by now I did not care what happened. I knew I was going to be dropped so that I was hardly disappointed when I was. I thought that if a player had the ability and had scored runs in the past, then they would at least allow more than one match to pass before finding an alternative. The West Indian selectors obviously felt there was no point in persisting with me, although yet again they did not give me either an explanation or advice. My depression and disappointment were aggravated by a quote from Lloyd in a Sydney

134

paper which indicated that I was now only on the tour for my catching. This upset me desperately and if I had had a choice, I would have gone home there and then. I felt my problems were only technical ones which could have been ironed out by someone more experienced than myself. The pace in the wicket and the extra bounce were consistently my undoing and I did not have a clue how to rectify it. Maybe I should have gone to Lloyd and asked him what I should do to counteract these basic faults. I was playing like an English player and paying the penalty, but the more I mulled it all over and disappeared deeper into myself, the less easy it became to speak to anyone.

I was 12th man at Sydney again and after we had made 355, Greg Chappell scored an unbeaten 182, courtesy of Keith Boyce, who dropped him early on, and they led by 50 on the first innings. Sydney, of course, was the scene of the Ian Chappell incident when he was out but refused to budge, and the series effectively ended there and then with the umpire's decision. It may sound like an excuse or a facile judgement, but I believe it to be true. Thomson took 6 second innings wickets against a demoralised side and a target of 79 caused them only momentary problems. The series now stood at 3–1 to Australia and it is true to say that many of the party, like me, wanted to go home. There was simply no point in continuing.

By now, I had accepted it would need a run of injuries to get me back in, so that I became little more than a passenger for the last four weeks of the tour. In Tasmania I made 76 and 62 in matches of no great stature and I thought there could be just an outside chance of a recall for the Fifth Test at Adelaide. Instead Viv Richards opened and once more I was 12th man. I think that had I been selected for Adelaide I would have issued an ultimatum. I would have said: give me two matches or none at all. The thought of a trial would have been too much and I was almost glad when my name did not appear in the team. My pal Holder bowled well at Adelaide to take 8 wickets in the match, but as a contest there was nothing in the match and centuries by Redpath, in the first, and Turner in the second, left us a huge 490 to win. Viv's 101 failed to

135

alter the inevitability of defeat and we lost by 190 runs.

The Sixth Test back at Melbourne was no more than a joke. Baichan was brought in, although not as an opener, and I was duly ignored for the third successive occasion. Redpath's 101 set up another big score for the Aussies and with Gilmour and Lillee each taking 5 wickets, we started the second innings 191 behind. McCosker for once succeeded with an unbeaten 109 and we were left with 492 to win. It was all over early on the fifth day; Australia had beaten us by 165 runs and by 5-1 in the series.

Never have I been more glad to head for home. I could not get out of Australia fast enough and I suspect many of my colleagues felt the same. Newspaper stories saying how poorly we had played and how weak we had turned out to be only added to our remorse. The tour had been a terrible disaster for me and there could not have been any more than half a dozen of my colleagues who left Australia with their heads held high. We felt we had let ourselves, the West Indies, our supporters and the Aussies down, and we limped home a dejected crew.

The tour had taught me a lesson, several lessons in fact. I resolved from now on to become such a consistently high scorer that I could not be ignored. The tour management had all that talent at their disposal and yet we still lost by an emphatic margin. They failed to get the best out of some of the best players in the world and undeniably, man for man, the best team. I acknowledge, for instance that a pair at Brisbane had put a question mark against my name. But why drop me after one poor match? And why bring me back for Melbourne? I had done nothing to warrant a return. These sorts of things mystified me.

With the tour to England scheduled for the summer of 1976, I was in urgent need of runs. I went back to Barbados and scored my first century for them against Jamaica, and never has a century been more welcome. There was time also for me to propose to Anita and my depression disappeared when she agreed to marry me. With a century for Barbados also, I was in a much better frame of mind when I was chosen for the tour of England. After the failures of Australia, it was imperative that I succeeded in

Vanburn Holder (right) and Lawrence Rowe (left) join me in getting a closer look at the Australians at an animal sanctuary in Queensland

Jack Nicklaus beware. Gordon Greenidge, occasional golfer, takes part in a sportsmen's tournament at Indooroopilly, Australia

Time to relax . . . a few drinks with, among others, Roy Fredericks (with cigarette) and Clive Lloyd (partly hidden)

conditions and in places familiar to me. The alternative was obvious enough: the end of my Test career before it had really begun. That was all the incentive I needed.

After Australia, India were scheduled to visit the West Indies. It soon became obvious that I was not in favour because the nearest I got to a place in the five Tests was being named as 12th man for the match in Barbados. I returned to England early with my fingers firmly crossed.

11 Making Hay in an English Summer

England and the summer tour of 1976 represented a major new challenge for me. The comparative lack of success in the World Cup of the preceeding summer and the downright failures of the winter in Australia had left a question mark over my head. In English domestic cricket I had become one of the most respected and feared players on the circuit, but in order to satisfy myself and the growing number of people who had watched the stutter in my progress, I had to use this tour to prove I was a player of international class. The chance to play a full series 'at home' in England so soon after my Australian debacle could not have been better timed. It provided an immediate opportunity to redeem myself and I was grateful to see my name in the tour party. After the disasters of Australia, it was hardly surprising when the selectors announced five new names in the party from that which had surrendered so abjectly Down Under. Lance Gibbs, arguably the best spin bowler ever produced by the West Indies, had retired after overhauling Freddie Trueman to become the leading wicket-taker in the history of Test cricket. Keith Boyce was something of a surprise omission and there were no places for the reserve wicketkeeper David Murray, Len Baichan and the left-arm spinner Inshan Ali. Their replacements were the all-rounder Collis King, Larry Gomes of Trinidad and Middlesex, the wicketkeeper Mike Findlay, Raphick Jumadeen, a spinner from Trinidad and in Wayne Daniel another Barbadian fast bowler to add to what was already a formidable array of fast-bowling talent. The full party was: Clive Lloyd (Guyana, captain), Deryck Murray (Trinidad, vice-captain), Wayne Daniel (Barbados), Mike Findlay (Combined Islands), Roy Fredericks (Guyana), Larry Gomes (Trinidad). Gordon Greenidge (Barbados), Vanburn Holder (Barbados), Mike Holding (Jamaica), Bernard Julien (Trinidad), Raphick Jumadeen (Trinidad), Alvin Kallicharran (Guyana), Collis King (Barbados), Albert Padmore (Barbados), Viv Richards (Combined Islands), Andy Roberts (Combined Islands) and Lawrence Rowe (Jamaica). Many of that squad played or had played in county cricket and so the conditions and the wickets were familiar to all but a few of us. It was by now an experienced party with plenty of quality batsmen and with a heavy emphasis on pace bowlers. Without Gibbs we were short of top-class spinners, but we were hoping that with so many quicks there would be no need to use either Padmore nor Jumadeen too much. For my own part, there was so much to prove. This time I did not get carried away with the belief that because I knew so much of cricket in England there would be nothing to stop me making a hatful of runs. I was well aware that bowlers like John Snow, Peter Lever and the other prospective England pace bowlers knew all about my weaknesses and my penchant for attacking and they were clever enough to expose them. My failures had taught me humility, but there was absolutely no chance of my changing my attitude towards batting and cricket in general. However, there was one, very basic, alteration in my attitude towards the West Indian team and its method of selection. The board of control has such curious ways, I suppose to appease so many voices from so many different islands, that for all our talent, some of the teams appear to have been chosen by lottery. As I saw it, if I did not get runs for myself then I would be out of the team no matter the result. I had to justify my selection with a continual succession of big scores so that there were no excuses to leave me out again.

From the moment I learned that I was in the party to tour England, I made up my mind to make the needs of the team secondary to the needs of Gordon Greenidge. It may sound selfish and even childish, possibly both, but that was how I felt and I make no apologies. What may surprise you is that I still have the

139

same attitude to cricket fundamentally, although it has been tempered by success of recent years. I knew for instance, that I could not confide in Clive Lloyd nor ask for his advice. He had done nothing to help or reassure me in Australia, reserving his comments about me for the newspapers or for team meetings when he dished out nothing but criticism. The board itself had chosen Clyde Walcott and Frankie Thomas as the tour managers and they were a big improvement on the management in Australia. Clyde was calm, clear and utterly sensible and Frankie gave us all individual help and the reassurance so lacking in the past. It made for a much better spirit in the camp and for someone like me who needs the confidence of others, a tremendous boost and a major reason why the tour was such a personal success. Three Test centuries, all made in succession, and nearly 2,000 runs on the tour added up to my finest hour and established me, once and for all, as one of the world's top opening batsmen. It might have been supposed from my, almost daily, success, that I would have been popular among my team-mates but I do not think, apart from a few expectations, that I ever was.

My depression and moodiness in Australia may have had something to do with their reaction, but in any case, I did not feel inclined to do anything other than go my own way when we began the tour. After India and after Australia, being in England gave me much greater freedom. Not knowing the other countries, it was hard to get away alone for anything other than a few hours in one of the cars made available to the team. In England it was possible for me to get down the motorways to see Anita or to simply be alone and to free myself of the tensions of the tour. Vanburn Holder, my closest friend, was aware of how I felt and how some of my colleagues felt towards me. As a result, I did not feel especially welcome in the company of some of them and I was quite prepared to head off to discos on my own, or with Anita when I was able to get down to London to see her. A curious atmosphere, then, surrounding a series which I think I can say without contradiction was dominated by Viv Richards, Mike Holding and myself. England, under Tony Greig's control, were beaten 3–0 in the Tests and as heavily overwhelmed as we had been a few months earlier in Australia. Greig, of course, provided one of the most memorable quotes of the cricketing year when he said he was going to make the West Indians grovel. With all its connotations, it was a comment designed to stir us up and I can tell him now that he succeeded. Personally, I had grovelled enough in my life and I was not prepared to do so to him and a badly balanced England team. His words acted as a spur to me and I believe they had much the same effect on many of my team-mates. Since his involvement with Packer, Greig has been heavily derided in England by its cricket supporters, the same people who welcomed him with open arms when they realised he was not necessarily barred by his South African birth.

I believe Greig did a good job as skipper of an England side which was probably as weak as at any time since the war. I do not think he was ever any more than an ordinary player but his Test record is a good one and it was not his fault that the teams he led were, for the most part, a class or two below their major rivals. As a captain he was as shrewd and as capable as any in the world game, probably only Ian Chappell seriously rivalling him. We knew he had a way with words and his 'grovelling' comment was not spoken off the top of his head. The consensus of opinion in the West Indies dressing room was that Greig had said the words for a purpose, a calculated comment. Looking back, though, I'm not sure what his intentions were. Was he trying to make us so mad as to panic? Or was he trying to make his team that much better than they really were? Whatever his aims, we went on to slaughter England with only the minimum of resistance from hardened battlers like Underwood, Knott, Amiss, Greig himself and veteran performers like David Steele and Brian Close, who had been summoned from their cricketing dotages to face our fearsome fast bowlers with little more than their raw courage. I wish I could say that, on the whole, England were difficult opponents but, after Australia, it was like playing against schoolchildren and apart from occasional minor embarrassments the tour passed off without any of the exhausting dramas of my previous two tours. I have no

141

wish to belittle fellow professionals nor to denigrate my own achievements, but England really did not extend us as much as we had feared and our ultimate victory was as hollow as it was emphatic. Nevertheless, it was a tour of triumph for me.

Although I had expected to be chosen for the tour because of my knowledge of England and its players, I was by no means certain of a place after my poor form in Australia. On returning from Barbados I took the precaution of playing a Benson and Hedges match for Hampshire while the West Indian selectors deliberated over the squad. Not surprisingly, there was a feeling of relief from myself whan I found my name among the tourists because genuine fears that my Test career may be over nagged at me in the weeks before the party was announced. For that reason, it was a vital tour and I had to do well.

With my season with Hampshire over after only one match, I joined the West Indian party and early in May at one of the prettiest cricket grounds in the world, Arundel Castle, I made 84 in our opening match against the Duchess of Norfolk's XI. At this stage of the season any big score was welcome, even in the leisurely atmosphere of a minor representative match. A week later we were at Southampton to play Hampshire, where neither Roberts nor myself were chosen, although I think both of us would have relished playing against our county, weakened as they were by injuries. Two failures against Kent did my cause no good at all and it became important for me to make runs against MCC at Lords, in what amounted to a Test trial for many of the England players. Richard Gilliat was the MCC captain and in their first innings he was one of the few players to show any resolution against our fast bowlers in making 66. In the second innings he was not so successful, making only 3 before being caught by Greenidge. I made only 5 in our second innings but in the first I top-scored with 82 and I felt as if a huge weight had been lifted from my shoulders. I had virtually played my way back into the Test team.

The innings at Lords gave me fresh confidence and a second-innings score of 115 against Somerset at Taunton in our next match virtually booked my place for the First Test at Trent Bridge.

Comparatively low scores at Hove in a drawn match with Sussex did no harm to my prospects and I was elated naturally when the team was announced with me as partner to Fredericks at number two in the order. My familiarity with English conditions and their players lessened my anxiety as the day approached and I remember feeling relaxed and ready when the series began in the first few days of June in what turned out to be a beautiful summer. Unquestionably, England feared our fast bowlers and the press can have done nothing for their confidence by continually highlighting our strong points and denigrating the England players' ability to deal with not only the fast bowlers but also our multitude of attacking batsmen. It may have been panic, it may have been reasoned judgement but England recalled the durable veteran Brian Close and, with solid defensive players like David Steele and John Edrich already in residence, the English policy was clearly aimed at blunting the pace with the straightest of straight bats.

We batted first and, thanks to Viv Richards, who made a colossal 232, and Alvin Kallicharran (97) we went on to make an impregnable 494 against a by no means unimpressive bowling line-up of Snow, Hendrick, Old, Greig, Woolmer and Underwood. Richards and Kallicharran put on 303 for the third wicket and English fears about our batting capabilities were fully realised almost immediately. I wish I could say that I had made a significant contribution to this huge total. Sad to relate, Hendrick got rid of me for 22 and not for the first time in my life, I was forced to sit it out while others made batting look easy.

Mike Holding was not playing in this match but this was no excuse for our inability to run through what was only a moderate batting order. Bob Woolmer made 82, but the real stumbling-block was the grittily determined Steele, who got his head down for what seemed like days to defy everything hurled at him by men like Roberts, Daniel, Julien and Holder. He was out eventually for 106 and England, at 332 all out, were in a good enough position to ensure safety. The wicket was causing no real problems and although we lost Fredericks early on, I was moving along impressively until, on reaching 23, I gave Chris Old a return catch. Once

143

again, Richards led the way and we were able to declare, leaving England something approaching 350 to win with no realistic chance of actually doing so. Edrich and Close dug in after 2 wickets had gone down cheaply and the match was drawn to the intense satisfaction of the English, who had come out of the match rather better than they had anticipated. Obviously, I would have wanted a few more runs from the match but I felt there was nothing about the bowling to worry me and I figured that as long as I did enough to retain my place, then the runs would surely come. I made sure of staying in the team by scoring 72 and 86 at Old Trafford in the 6 wicket win over Lancashire, and my name was duly pencilled in for the Second Test at Lords.

Holding was back in the West Indian team, and in calling up the spin of Jumadeen, Wayne Daniel was omitted. How England must have envied our wealth of talent in the face of such an extravagant gesture of cricketing opulence. I could see no reason why, with a fair rub of the green, I could not make a big score or two here at Lords. It had been a ground on which I had always managed to acquit myself creditably in the past and I was looking forward to the action.

England batted first and with Roberts taking 5 wickets, were all out for 250. Brian Close battled hard for 60 but the total was little more than ordinary and we could see no reason why we could not build a substantial first-innings lead. Our hopes were dashed quickly. Fredericks, Gomes and Kallicharran were all back in the pavilion with only 40 on the board. It was than that Clive Lloyd and I came together to provide the only stable partnership of the innings. We put on 99 for the fourth wicket before another collapse saw us lose our last 7 wickets for 43. Lloyd made 50 but I was playing with confidence and vigour and at 84, should have gone on to record a century. With a well-deserved century beckoning, Derek Underwood dismissed me and we were 68 in arrears, instead of being comfortably in front. The innings boosted my confidence and my self-belief, and made me realise that providing I stayed clear of injury, there were plenty of runs for the making in this series. The onus was on me.

Steele and Close continued their defiance of our pace men with solid and sensible grafting and although Roberts took five more wickets, we were asked to chase 323. Fredericks played outstandingly to score a century but a personal total of 22 represented something of a disappointment after dominating the first innings so emphatically. The match was drawn with us still well adrift of our target and England finding our depth of batting too much for their depleted bowling. Two Tests and two draws scarcely represented an achievement from the West Indies point of view. We had expected to be at least one up and our failure to do so was something of an irritation. England were quite delighted, especially as they had the better of the Lords Test.

It was while playing at Lords in the Second Test that one of the more unusual incidents of my career took place. I lifted one delivery for six, although I am not sure who was bowling, and it hit some old lady hard on the leg. I was unaware of anyone being hurt but apparently Mrs Grace Mendoza needed hospital treatment for her injury. Mrs Mendoza did not blame me for what had happened, but she asked if she could meet the nasty man who had inflicted this discomfort upon her. *The Sun* took a picture of us together and I offered my belated apologies. She was very good about it and insisted there was no question of any blame. She said she just wanted to meet me and talk about the match which, in the circumstances, was the least I could do. At 67 she told me she enjoyed watching the West Indies batting and she ended up by wishing me well for the rest of the series. Perhaps her wishes had magical properties because the following two Test matches were the most productive of my career.

My build up to Old Trafford and the Third Test could hardly have been better. An unbeaten 101 against Leicestershire was my best score but I was at my peak of form and fitness and raring to follow up the comparative success of Lords. England brought in Mike Selvey for his first Test and he made a sensational start when it was decided that we should bat first on a wicket which was helping the seamers. Selvey sent back Fredericks, Richards and Kallicharran with an inspired spell of swing bowling and with

145

Mike Hendrick accounting for Lloyd, we were in deep trouble at 26 for 4 and the large Lancastrian crowd baying for more. In such a perilous position so much depended on how I was able to cope and survive. Collis King was my partner now, inexperienced in Test cricket and unused to having to defend for his life. This was the moment I had been waiting for. All the big names gone and so much resting on me.

England tried every conceivable variation to part us but with a mixture of fortune and dogged resistance, we clung on and the runs started to come a little more fluently. I had made 26 when I had my one piece of luck. I was dropped off a not-very-difficult chance and I celebrated by hitting the next three balls for fours. On I went, past my 50 and with King providing support at the other end, put on 111 for the fifth wicket of which his share was a valuable 32.

Apart from the dropped catch, I never felt in any real trouble and as long as others could stay with me a reasonable total was not impossible. I do not recall the exact delivery on which I reached my ton or anything like that, but I remember sailing through the 90s without any bother and through to my century. Wickets continued to fall at regular intervals and, apart from myself, King and Wayne Daniel, who made ten, no other player reached double figures. Derek Underwood eventually bowled me when I had made 134 but it failed to stop me receiving a standing ovation from the generous crowd and from enjoying my finest moment. The West Indies were all out for 211 so that my contribution had been absolutely crucial to the team performance and represented a major triumph. England had left us off the hook, and me in particular, so that when they came to bat, they were soon in the depths of despair. Steele resisted as only he can for long enough to make 20 but Daniel, Roberts and Holding caused havoc and they were all out for 71. This not only spelled ruination for the English but it made my performance of the day before look superhuman. Since we were required to bat again against a demoralised side, I could see no reason not to make another big score. This is exactly what happened. The pitch was now playing easier and, Selvey and Hendrick rendered useless by it, Underwood and Pocock were required to wheel away for hour after unproductive hour.

Roy Fredericks hit his wicket when he had made 50 but Richards and I grew in confidence and power while England's morale collapsed correspondingly and visibly. After the terrible disappointment of India, where a run out had denied me a century in each innings, the thought struck me as I neared my second hundred of the match that I must not be too careless. No one was more relieved than me when I finally passed the ton mark. Soon afterwards, with my score at 101, Selvey bowled me but at 224 for 2, the West Indies were perfectly placed to strike for victory. Only the great George Headley had ever scored a century in each innings against England for the West Indies and the thought of joining one of the game's immortals only added to my delight. I believe now that my desire to prove something to the West Indies— players, management and supporters alike—had much to do with my double success at Old Trafford. At last I had proved to them all that I was a player fit to be ranked with the best, and that their treatment of me in Australia was totally unjustified. I felt like telling them individually: 'Look at the scoreboard.' My critics were silenced for once and, I hoped, for all. After the years of struggle and the mental torment of my failures, the hours after the completion of my second century have to be among the finest of my life as I wallowed in the glow of self-congratulation and the congratulations of others. Viv continued the demolition of the toiling England attack and with Clive declaring at 411 for 5, the chance to go one up in the series was very real indeed. England were by now a dispirited and disillusioned outfit and once more our three fast bowlers ripped through the minimum resistance and at 126 all out, we were home and dry by a resounding 425 runs. With their first defeat in three matches and two to play, England sensed that they just did not have the class to compete as equals and it was up to us to capitalise.

I celebrated my achievement by scoring 117 and 60, albeit against Ireland in Dublin and the stage was set for the Fourth Test at Headingley, with my prestige as high as it had ever been.

I saw no reason to alter my approach when the series moved on to Headingley. If I scored runs, the team benefited, but if the team scored runs and I did not, then through past experience, I knew that they would soon find a replacement, however well I had done earlier. England, so outplayed at Old Trafford, were beginning to look around for a bright new generation of players to lift them from the gloom of almost continual failure recently against ourselves and the Australians. Frank Hayes was retained, despite his poor scores at Old Trafford, Bob Willis came back as the bowling spearhead and Chris Balderstone was given his Test debut at the age of 35, after years of consistency at county level. None of these changes disturbed our calm belief in our capabilities as a team and when Lloyd won the toss and Fredericks and I went out to bat, there was not the slightest hint of anxiety. Like a man in a rich vein of good form, I carried on where I had left off at Old Trafford, middling each ball without fear of the consequences and with Fredericks doing much the same at the other end, it was not until the score had reached 192 that we were parted. Fredericks was out for 109, but in the company of Viv Richards I went on to make 115 and to give us the basis for another big score. It sounds blasé, but I just took it all as it came, using the years of graft in county cricket as my platform for countering the combined wiles of Snow, Underwood, Ward, Willis and whoever else Greig in desperation threw at us.

As a sort of celebration, although I was not aware of it at the time, I hit a six against Underwood into the football stand at Headingley to give me 500 runs for the series. I suppose this was more than I could have expected when it all began, but with a maximum of three innings to go, there was plenty of opportunity for more runs. The West Indies were out for 450 and Tony Greig and Alan Knott each scored centuries for England to leave them only 63 behind after our pace men had again threatened to run through them easily. Alan Ward had me leg before for 6 in the second innings and with only Collis King (58) making any runs, England suddenly found themselves with only 260 to beat us and time enough in which to do it.

So much depended on their nerve as much as on our bowling,

but Steele, Hayes and Balderstone were out quickly and at 23 for 3, a golden chance to equalise the series seemed to be slipping away from them. As usual, Roberts had done the crucial damage in removing all three and in spite of pockets of resistance from Woolmer, Willey on his Test debut and Tony Greig, who was still there on 76 when the last wicket went down, we were victors by 55 runs. Once more, England's inability to deal with consistently fast and hostile bowlers had been exposed and the inquests continued for days in the English papers.

Our second Test victory made the last of the series at the Oval little short of meaningless as far as we were concerned, which is just as well because my contribution towards a West Indies total of 687 for 8 declared was a duck. Bob Willis had me leg before wicket and I was left to rue my failure as Viv Richards dominated the match with a personal score of 291, with everyone else taking advantage of an easy-paced wicket to make runs. Dennis Amiss battled hard in scoring 203 but Alan Knott apart, received precious little support and at 435 all out, they were well adrift of us.

Batting a second time, I was a little more cautious and in making 85 not out, we were able to declare at 182 for no wicket, to leave England a massive 435 to win. The task was clearly beyond them, and Michael Holding added 6 more wickets to the 8 he took in the first innings as England folded to a 231 run defeat to compound a disastrous series for them. In five Tests they used 21 players without ever finding the right formula and, deprived of Geoff Boycott's services by his own reluctance, they had neither the technique nor the talent to deal with our fast bowlers. Apart from Underwood, they did not have the bowlers either to do anything other than contain people like myself and Richards for short spells. Added to the fact that crucial catches were put down you have an England side in 1976 that was simply not good enough to cause us a moment's worry and I should think it must rank, on the whole, as among the poorest of England outfits.

For me, it was the year in which I came of age. Nearly 2,000 tour runs and a Test average of 65.77 represented a huge contrast in my fortunes with Australia. At last I had justified my ability in the very place where it had all begun and there was no more delighted and fulfilled cricketer than I at the end of the summer of 1976. My reputation had been made and my international future assured, and I headed for the West Indies in a much happier frame of mind than when I had arrived in the spring. With the Pakistanis touring the West Indies and with a full winter ahead playing for Barbados, there was much to look forward to.

Not the least of my rewards for an outstanding season was the honour of being named as one of *Wisden's* five cricketers of the year. *Wisden* is the cricketing bible and to be chosen by them is something every player cherishes. The honour did not just provide me with a free copy of the book. It recognised my talents and my contribution to the game of that particular summer and for that I will always be grateful. The selection is made world-wide and it meant that in a matter of six or eight months I had developed from what amounted to a fringe Test player, never quite sure of my place, to full-blown international star. Unquestionably, the summer had provided a major breakthrough in my career and I was left wondering how much my new, some would say selfish, attitude had been responsible for my sudden and startling development.

I may even have made myself a little unpopular with some of the other West Indian players and my 'Go-it-alone' lifestyle may not have been the ideal approach to a tour where integration and team spirit are considered of paramount importance. I resolved to continue my policy and, to this day, have had absolutely no cause to regret it. I am not saying every player should take the same narrow view. All I am saying is that it worked for me in a manner I could never have anticipated and I shall adopt it until I take my pads off for the last time on behalf of the West Indies.

12 Chasing Pirate Gold

Pakistan were scheduled to tour the West Indies in the winter of 1976–7 and I was determined to use the opportunity to silence my West Indian critics once and for all. Having achieved so much in England during the summer of 1976, I was as sure of my place in the team as at any stage in my career and it was up to me to get enough big scores to end the anti-Greenidge feeling which still persisted around the islands in spite of my success. In fact my run of hundreds against England would have merely confirmed the view of the majority that I was 'an English player'. Certainly I am prepared to admit that only one century for Barbados in three seasons had done nothing to dispel the antagonism. The Barbadians still found it easier to identify with someone like Desmond Haynes, latterly my opening partner for both Barbados and the West Indies, than they did with me. He had been born and raised in the island; people in the crowd knew him and his family, whereas my three winters in Barbados had done little to get rid of the notion of me as an itinerant, mercenary cricketer who just happened to have born in their island. Probably even Geoff Greenidge, a white man, was better received by the local crowds simply because they knew him. It was against that sort of background that I returned to the West Indies for the Pakistan series, determined to prove to them all that I was a player of quality who deserved their support, recognition and applause.

The first of the five Tests took place on my home ground, the Kensington Oval at Bridgetown and it needed a desperate last wicket stand between Andy Roberts and a young pace bowler, Colin Croft, to save us from going one down immediately. Joel Garner and Vanburn Holder were the only other Barbadians in the

151

team and my scores of 47 and 2 can have done little to win over my critics among the crowd.

Set to score 306 in the fourth innings, Sarfraz, Imran and Salim had us in some trouble and at 237 for 9 we had come to expect the inevitable. But Roberts and Croft batted out time and denied Pakistan victory and an important blow to our morale. I only wish I had been able to make a big score in front of my own supporters and detractors alike.

The Second Test at Port of Spain, Trinidad, gave me a new chance and it was on the spinners' paradise of Queens Park that scores of 5 and 70 set up a chance for us to win by 6 wickets and inched me closer to my ambition of a Test century in the West Indies. Inconsistent batting by the Pakistanis left us only just over 200 to win and my score of 70 was instrumental in us winning rather more easily than we should have done on a wicket as helpful as ever to the spinners. Curiously enough, the wickets vary considerably in the West Indies. Port of Spain has nurtured a succession of good spinners; Barbados gets slower as the match progresses; in Jamaica anything can happen, but the best batting track is unquestionably the Bourda at Georgetown in Guyana. It was to Georgetown that we went for the third of the matches against Pakistan with our expectations high after winning in Trinidad. The match turned out to be a triumph for me but at the same time represented one of my greatest disappointments.

Roberts, Garner and Croft had them all out for 194. Fredericks soon went, but in the company of first Richards and then Kallicharran I took my score to 91 before the occasional spin of Majid was responsible for my dismissal. I was furious; so near and yet so far from holding my bat aloft and being able to say to the West Indian public: 'I told you so.'

A big lead of 254 left the Pakistanis with plenty of batting to do if they were to save themselves from defeat. With so many good batsmen, they could not fail a second time and they did not. They were all out for 540 and with little time in which to get 287, Fredericks and I used the opportunity for some batting practice. I was soon outscoring Fredericks and after 24 overs I suddenly

Prudential World Cup 1979: on my way to a century against India at
Edgbaston (*Ken Kelly, Birmingham*)

Clive Lloyd holds the 1979 Prudential World Cup aloft as we celebrate our victory over England in the final. Left to right the players are: Marshall, Richards, Croft, Garner, King, Holding, Lloyd, Kallicharran, Deryck Murray and look who's holding the champagne. (*Ken Kelly, Birmingham*)

found myself needing only a few runs for the century I had so sorely missed in the first innings. Imran was the bowler and it was just about the last over of the match. I had made 96 and the score stood at 154 for no wicket. Time was running out as I went to turn Imran to leg where an inviting gap lay open. If I had connected properly, it was a certain four and my century also. But, as so often happens, I did not quite time the ball in my anxiety and Haroon Rashid dived to hold a magnificent catch. With my agonising dismissal, the match ended as a draw.

For the Fourth Test we returned to Port of Spain and, for the first time, the depth of the Pakistan batting proved too much. Mushtaq scored a century for them in the first innings and it says little for our reply that I was second highest scorer with 32. We trailed by 187 on the first innings and, seizing their chance admirably, Pakistan increased this by sensible batting to 488. There was little we could do except try to bat for a draw, but with Sarfraz, Wasim Raja and Mushtaq each taking 3 wickets, we slumped to defeat by 266 runs to the dismay of the players and the gallery of fans at Queens Park. My own total of 11 had turned it into a match best forgotten from my point of view and I was left with just one more Test match, at Kingston in Jamaica, in which to set the record straight.

Jamaica is a beautiful island but it has massive problems of poverty and lawlessness. It is unlike anywhere else in the West Indies and Jamaicans, similarly, are not like other West Indians in their attitude to life and the way they live it. It is a dangerous place and not even the cricket ground is safe from riots, damage, looting and whatever. The Jamaicans do know their cricket; they love the game and they love great players, especially if they come from Jamaica. In the years that I had played in the West Indies, both in Tests and for Barbados, they had been the slowest to accept me. They did not believe I had quality and saw me, I'm sure, as a batsman who liked to attack every ball, but who did not have the ability to adjust if the conditions were not right. They were my sternest critics and with the series poised at 1–1 it was by no means the ideal place for me to come for the deciding Test.

In front of as noisy and as hostile a crowd as imaginable, the final match began with the West Indies batting first. Imran soon sent back Fredericks and Richards but for reasons for which I am still not able to account, every shot that I played came off the middle of the bat and the applause, minimal to begin with, grew in intensity and volume as I raced past 50 and on towards my hundred. Noting, it seemed, could stop me and although my colleagues were having their troubles, no bowler could halt my flow. I must have been in my late 70s when I had my one piece of luck. Sikander was the bowler and I hit the ball straight to silly mid-off where Asif Iqbal dropped a simple chance. I breathed a sigh of relief and raced away to my century. The applause was deafening and, on coming out soon afterwards, I lapped up the music of the cheering. At last I had proved to these people that I was not just a flashy English batsman. I was a world-class player and now they knew it.

It was another of the great moments of my career, but even now there is still a feeling in the West Indies which runs against me. I think, in spite of my years as a West Indian Test player and my winters with Barbados, that they do not accept me purely because of the years spent away from the Caribbean. They still regard me as an outsider, somehow intruding on their territory or their private party and I do not think there is anything that I can do to change this attitude. The West Indian public are the first to congratulate me if things are going well, like that famous day in Kingston, but for the rest of the time their indifference borders on hostility. In a nutshell, I believe they do not rate me as a cricketer and I do not think there will ever be anything I can do to alter their views.

It is as well, though, that a certain, now notorious character thought differently about my ability. Kerry Packer first intruded upon my life at around the time the West Indies were involved in the series with Pakistan. I had heard via the dressing-room grapevine that Roberts, Holding and Viv Richards had put their signatures to a document binding them exclusively to what later became known as a cricketing circus. The players concerned were saying nothing, under orders, about the venture, but the word got around that the rewards were high. At that stage I did not know what sort of shape this 'circus' was going to take but I heard that it involved Australia and television. There may have been one other West Indian player who, at this time, had signed for Packer although I am not sure who. Naturally this new and exciting-sounding venture aroused more than curiosity and the first reaction of us all was how to get in on it.

I was by now recently engaged and destined to be married in six months. My thoughts had already turned to finding ways of using the winters profitably since there were not always going to be tours and from past experience, I knew there was absolutely no guarantee that I would be on them anyway. In short, I was looking for a better and more lucrative way of filling the months between the domestic county seasons and Packer could not have come along at a more opportune time.

This is something the anti-Packer factions should realise, because there were many so-called top cricketers like myself for whom the winters were potentially six-month-long nightmares. The counties did not, and still do not, find us employment and we are left to our own devices. I have been lucky comparatively because there always seem to have been West Indian tours or stints in Barbados to occupy me, but I know from many of my colleagues that the winter can often mean only the dole or fill-in jobs. How I spent the winter I regarded as my business and a commercial opportunity such as the one being dangled in front of us by Packer and his henchmen was too good to miss. Packer had obviously decided that the tour by Pakistan offered him the chance to sign up the leading West Indian players and after my disaster in Australia little more than a year previously, I was not surprised when my name was not the first they sought. Since only three or possibly four had actually committed themselves to Packer, I returned to England for the 1977 season with Hampshire and thought no more about it. So little did I consider the subject that through Andy Roberts was sharing a flat with me, it never occurred to me to tackle him about it and he, for his part, certainly never ventured any information. As with most subjects, he was keeping quiet.

The rumours about this new enterprise grew as the season progressed and it came to my attention that Barry Richards was also a signatory. We were playing Surrey at the club ground at Guildford and it was particularly successful for me because I scored 200 in a match which we lost. I asked Barry then if he had heard much about this man Packer and his commercial cricket circus. Barry admitted that he had signed and, as a man starved of the big-time by the ban on South Africa, was viewing the prospect with some excitement. I asked him if there was any prospect of getting me in because the more I was hearing about it, the more I wanted to join. He told me that some of Packer's men were in London, staying at the Dorchester Hotel and that he would be prepared to take me there. At the end of a day's play at Guildford, the two of us drove the 30 or 40 miles to the Dorchester where I was ushered into the presence of Andrew Caro, then Packer's number one aide. Caro was honest about it all. He told me that it was the intention of Packer to sign all the world's leading players to play in Australia, largely for the benefit of his television station, Channel Nine. Caro went on to tell me about how fierce the competition would be, because the depth of talent was so great. But when we got round to talking about the financial rewards, I was staggered. I had heard that the money was good, but never did I expect it to be quite as good as the terms he offered me in his room at the hotel. Within half an hour of first shaking his hand, I was shaking it again—this time in agreement to his offer. Literally 30 minutes after arriving full of anticipation at the Dorchester, I was a Packer player and let me say, here and now, never once did I have cause to regret it.

The money was exceptional by the standards cricketers had come to expect. It is no secret what some players were being paid by Packer and as an ordinary member of his 'circus' I was earning in the region of 25,000 Australian dollars a year plus allowances for working three winters for his pirate programme. When I put pen to paper in 1977 that 25,000 dollars meant something like £16,000

156

and I am giving no secrets away when I reveal that this is roughly four times what I was earning in the English summers. This is in no way a criticism of Hampshire who, after all, were only paying me the going rate but it must have been as much an eye-opener to them and the other counties as it was to me. Truth to tell, I would have signed for a lot less and I came away from the Dorchester with my head reeling from the astounding sums being talked of by Caro and the rest of the Packer associates. I remember thinking back to the toil and sweat of the tour of England only a year previously when, for a summer of five Tests and a full round of county matches for the West Indies, I was paid about £3,000. With such colossal sums being paid out by Packer the thought occurred to me more than once that cricket could never be quite the same again, no matter how soon the new 'war' between the game's authorities and Packer was settled. Soon afterwards, all hell broke loose as Packer and the TCCB squared up to each other and for the first time I came to realise the full implications of what I had done. There was talk of Packer players being banned for life, from everything except their own unique brand of cricket. There was talk of county players refusing to play with us and with the furore growing in intensity, I became deeply worried that I had signed away my livelihood to a bounty hunter for nothing other than a quick profit.

As the row brewed and as accusation was met by counter-accusation, I and my fellow Packer men at Hampshire—Barry Richards and Andy Roberts—went about our business as best we could in the circumstances. Only Barry knew I had signed for Packer and not even my flatmate, Roberts, was aware that I had followed his example and nailed my colours to the pirate's mast. It was not easy keeping the news to myself, especially as cricket lovers around the country came to the conclusion that I would surely be approached by Packer sooner or later. As a result, my mail at home and that addressed to me at the county ground grew bigger by the day with people I had never met imploring me not to be tempted by his bottomless purse. Hampshire supporters would stop me and tell me the same thing: Do not sign for Packer. How could I tell them that I had already committed myself to his cause? At this stage my feelings were divided. I did not want to upset so many people who had the game at heart and, more to the point, I did not want my county and Test career to be terminated purely because of what I saw only as a breakaway movement, playing for television, at loggerheads with the game's authorities who saw their sovereignty threatened. I prepared myself for the fact that I would probably never play Test cricket again. Curiously, I was ready to let that go by with no more than passing regret. I would have been hurt far more had I been banned from playing county cricket and I was both surprised and disappointed by the reaction of my Hampshire colleagues as I watched their attitude against Packer harden by the day. Eventually it became known, I know not how, that I had joined Packer and in some ways I was glad it was all out in the open. Some supporters registered their disapproval but others, less jaundiced, realised that cricket was my living and as one of its 'top' players was entitled to go about it in my own way. All I could do in the meanwhile was to get my head down and keeping playing to the best of my ability for Hampshire. It was the only way I knew.

While the debate and the recriminations continued, my game went from strength to strength, ironically, when it might so easily have fallen apart at the seams. Indeed, in terms of runs, 1977 was my best season for Hampshire thus far. I came third in the national averages and scored six centuries in 1,771 runs. Better still, I finished with an average of 61 which I had reason to regard as quite an achievement in the revolutionary circumstances. Twice I managed double centuries: an unbeaten 200 against Surrey and 208 at Headingley against Yorkshire and there were enough other big scores to justify Packer's faith in me and to quieten my critics among the Hampshire players and supporters. I also came top of Hampshire's John Player League averages and in the Benson and Hedges Cup earned Gold Awards for being man of the match against both Leicestershire and Gloucestershire, the latter after scoring a century. We reached the semi-finals of the Benson and Hedges Cup that year when at Southampton we started as favourites against Gloucestershire, a team we had already beaten convincingly in the same competition at the group qualifying stage. We fancied our chances of reaching the final of a major cup competition for the first time and a big crowd was optimistic when we dismissed them for 180. But that great South African competitor, Mike Proctor, bowling ferociously off his full run, took 4 wickets including mine in 5 balls, to have us in real trouble at 18 for 4. Turner and Nigel Cowley brought us back into the match again with a stand of 109 for the fifth wicket, but more wickets fell and at 159 for nine we were on the verge of defeat. Then Roberts, who seems to specialise in these cliff-hangers, was joined by Tom Mottram and they put on 14 for the last wicket. It was then, with 4 balls to go and with 8 needed for a dramatic victory, that Roberts was bowled. No final at Lords for Hampshire.

The Packer row reached the point of which the players' union were asked to vote on banning the Packer men from county cricket. I wanted to continue playing county cricket and I am still amazed by the number of people who believe that, in the company of Richards and Roberts, I voted for the motion dismissing us from the legitimate game. This is not so. Let me make the record correct now. I voted for us to stay in county cricket and I am only surprised that my county colleagues felt strongly enough to decide overwhelmingly that county cricket would be better off without the intrusion of the pirates.

Under what seemed almost a permanent cloud, I left for the first of my seasons with Packer late in 1977, truly looking forward to the challenge of his glamorous new competition. When we got there, we found that the WSC organisation was by no means completely ready for our arrival and the tour was slow to get off the ground. Packer's men looked after us well enough, but in such a revolutionary venture there were many teething problems and there seemed like days when no one understood what on earth we were supposed to be doing. The West Indian players received a shock immediately upon arrival. We were told that each of the three teams—Australia, West Indies and the World—were being designated a special team colour in which to play. To our horror, we discovered that we had been allocated a sort of coral pink (a shocking pink in this case), and several players lodged protests. In the West Indies, you see, pink has effeminate connotations and there were those among us who were not at all keen to wear our dashing new uniform.

There were days initially when we did not know if we were supposed to be coaching schoolchildren, playing a one-day match in an Outback cattle town or something more serious at one of the major Test venues. Eventually it all fell into place and although there was a tremendous amount of travelling and the crowds were slow to react, the series gradually began to win support and recognition from the Australian public. I imagine they wanted to be sure that the competition was real and that it was not somehow 'stage-managed'. With so much prize-money at stake and a genuine desire among the players to make it all work, the competition became as fierce as anything I had ever encountered in legitimate world cricket. There were so many good players and all of them wanting to do well that it was as hard, physically and mentally, as a full-blown county season rolled into three intense months. Unlike ordinary Test cricket where, after facing three good bowlers, there would be a couple below standard, WSC produced a steady stream of top-class bowlers, and the same too in the batting orders. The World XI, for instance, batted down to about number nine.

Floodlights and white balls came as a whole new world to us all, and although it was strange at first I, for one, soon came to enjoy playing under the lights, and some of my best performances came in the night matches. For me, the whole series provided a chance to erase the memories of the 1975-6 debacle and to avenge my failures. I resolved to make full use of the conditions in Australia, even if I did not score many runs. The Australians were as fiercely determined as ever and my form may have been indifferent, but a big century in Perth against them went some way to proving to myself that it was not impossible to get runs in Australia and to showing the public that I was a reasonable player after all.

In the strange surroundings of Melbourne's Australian Rules

Football ground, a disappointingly small crowd saw us beat the Australians in the first of the Supertests, a term which will mean little to those intrinsically opposed to Packer and all he stood for. Dennis Lillee continued his fine record against me by claiming my wicket in the first innings after I had made 22. He was not so fortunate in the second but my score of 16 was scarcely a success. Lillee got me again for 26 when we moved on to Sydney for the second Supertest. Our bowlers twice demolished them and we won by 9 wickets with myself unbeaten with 46 when the winning runs were scored. The third and last of the Supertests between the West Indies and the Australians took place at Adelaide where Australia gained some measure of revenge by beating us by 220 runs. I was reasonably satisfied with my first innings total of 40 but Lillee had me caught at first slip for nought early in the second innings. There was delight in the West Indies camp at winning the series 2–1, as much delight as there would have been had we overcome them in any official duel and I was pleased, as a measure of my progress, to be 'transferred' to the World XI for three more Supertests against the Australians. It was a little strange playing in such multi-national teams as those playing under the World XI banner but the team spirit was remarkably high and we blended into a convincing and successful unit.

At Sydney in the first of the Supertests between the World and Australia I found myself batting in the unfamiliar position of number three and made 23. In the second innings I was promoted to opener and renewed my partnership with Barry Richards. Could we now claim to be the world's best opening partnership?

I am pleased to report that Barry and I helped us build a big score and enabled us to go on and win by four wickets. Barry scored 48 and I made 50 and with Andy Roberts taking 6 second innings wickets, the Hampshire contingent could claim justifiably to have played an important part in the team's victory. My place was assured for the other two Supertests and it was on to Perth where in the second of the matches, I enjoyed my finest hour in Australia. At Gloucester Park, opposite the WACA, and where trotting (another of the great loves of Australians) takes place, they had somehow carved out a cricket wicket. Barry and I relished the occasion and, as if we were flaying some under-strength county side, put on 234 for the first wicket with the minimum of fuss. I had to go off at one time for repair to a minor injury but came back in again with the score at 481 for 3. Barry went on to make 207, Viv Richards weighed-in with 177 and I was out eventually for 140. That gave us a total of 625 and although Greg Chappell's 174 held us up for a while, we won the match by the satisfying margin of an innings and 73.

The third of the Supertests, back at the VFL in Melbourne, was little more than a formality. Greg Chappell made an unbeaten 246 and Rick McCosker 129 in an Australian total of 538 for 6. Viv's 170 helped us towards a respectable reply of 434. My own contribution was 46 and Barry scored 76. Joel Garner took 5 second innings wickets to have Australia all out for 167 but Lillee and Walker each took 5 in our second innings and we were beaten by 41 runs. This brought to a close a full and rewarding first season in Kerry Packer's many colours and there cannot have been a player among us who had not gained or learned something from a very arduous three or four months in the toughest of professional circuits.

The West Indian players returned home only to walk into the most tumultuous of rows. The West Indian Board of Control had decided to pick the Packer players for the impending Test series against the Australians, who, abiding by the ICC dictate, had chosen what amounted to their third best side, ignoring all their men committed to WSC. Bobby Simpson was brought out of many years' retirement to lead the young Australian team who, Jeff Thomson apart, were scarcely known outside their own states let alone internationally. On paper, it was hardly fair. The full West Indian team against a very youthful and not especially talented Australian outfit. The West Indian board incurred the wrath of the rest of the cricketing world for not standing firm against the creeping menace of Packer, but they went ahead and it was an extremely powerful, experienced and battle-hardened team which Clive Lloyd led into the First Test at Port of Spain. Needless to say, with a big crowd right behind us, Roberts, Garner and Croft cut through the raw Australian batting and they were all out for 90. Not even Thomson could stop us reaching 405 with all the major batsmen taking advantage of some tenacious but hardly venomous bowling. I made 43 but Kallicharran, a non-Packer man among us, hit 127 and with Roberts taking 5 wickets in the second innings, they gave us a huge and thoroughly predictable victory by an innings and 106 runs.

By now the Packer affair had reached the level of the courts of law and, despite protests, the WIBC chose much the same team for the Second Test at Bridgetown. Once again the Australians were outclassed, though not without a fight, and had little idea how to deal with our pace attack. It gave me great pleasure to be 80 not out when we won by 9 wickets in front of my home crowd. Two up and three Tests to play in the most one-sided of series. It all looked so easy but trouble was brewing and it all came to a head in Georgetown, Guyana, where the Third Test was to be played.

Richard Austin, Desmond Haynes and Colin Croft, all of whom had broken into the West Indian side for this series, were signed by Packer and their defection became public knowledge. Austin, Haynes and Deryck Murray were dropped immediately although no one quite knew why, and their absence angered the rest of us. We arrived in Georgetown and stayed at the Tower Hotel where we discovered we had been given no money and no allowances. Lloyd threatened to resign if Murray was not reinstated after what had seemed blatant discrimination. The board refused to back down and after a meeting at the nearby Pegasus Hotel, we voted to pull out en masse. Joel Garner and I returned to our hotel, not more than ten minutes away, where we discovered that our bags had been packed for us and were waiting in the lobby. What's more, a new alternative West Indian team were already in residence. The board had obviously expected us to pull out and had made plans in advance to replace us.

I flew back to Barbados at the end of a long and controversial winter. I had had only the minimum of rest since the end of the last English season, and a full winter of first Packer and then the two Tests against Australia had left me physically exhausted. There were still some games to be played for Barbados before returning to England and all I wanted to do was rest. With that in mind, I got in touch with the Barbadian authorities and volunteered to stand down from the Shell Shield matches. I was prepared to play if they really needed me, but they misconstrued my reasons for asking to be absent. They thought I was asking for more money in an oblique sort of way and I remember watching a television broadcast vilifying me for my action. They said I was too big for my boots and deserved to be ignored for ever. I can tell you, I was pleased to get back to England.

164

13 The War Continues

After the incredible sequence of events in the West Indies, it was time to get back to England in time for the start of the 1978 domestic season, but if I thought there would be a certain amount of light relief after a hectic and acrimonious winter, I was wrong. I was hoping, perhaps naively, that I would be able to get down to playing cricket and to be able, however temporarily, to forget about the political issues which were ripping the game apart. I thought it would be nice to return to the county circuit, and its own different demands, but the word Packer was still on the lips of every professional from Headingley to Southampton. I can only vouch for myself, although I am sure Richards and Roberts felt the same, but I was extremely tired after so many months of fiercely competitive cricket against the best players in the world. I believed that returning to the relatively tranquil pastures of Hampshire would help me rediscover my appetite and, make no mistake, I still wanted to play for the club. Richards and Roberts were different. Barry was now nearly thirty-three and after eleven county seasons, had reached the stage where he felt continuing any longer was pointless. He had nothing more to prove and, with a successful benefit behind him, could see no reason to stay on in England, a country to which he had no real loyalties. Barry had given the club tremendous service over the years but the winter with Packer had spoiled him. As a South African, he had played in only one Test series before his country had been barred from the international game. I honestly believe that the season with Packer, right at the end of his career, opened his eyes to what he had been missing and to what I had been taking for granted for the last four years. After encountering the best again, as if it were a Test series, he simply had no appetite any more for run-of-the-mill county matches played in front of tiny crowds. Hard as he tried to readjust, the parting of the ways had come and I suppose his exposure to Packer had a lot to do with his defection.

This too was the season in which Andy Roberts, the second of our three Packer men, decided that he could do without the drudgery of county cricket. I must come to Andy's defence because he is blamed wrongly for just walking out at a time when Hampshire needed him most. Andy was criticised by players and supporters alike for shirking his responsibility to Hampshire; for choosing his matches in which to play by feigning injury at the appropriate times. He had pulled out of several important matches when, late in 1978, he asked for his contract to be cancelled thereby giving up his chances of a lucrative benefit and also tearing up a rewarding contract. His reasons, then, for quitting could not have been trivial. After all, he was in the prime of his career and there was no alternative form of income on the horizon, certainly nothing which paid so well. Since I was sharing a flat with him I can vouch for the fact that he was not fit. He had several minor, nagging injuries but he complained of feeling unwell. The doctors were treating him for anaemia and his persistent demands for rest were beginning to irritate Gilliat and the Hampshire selectors. There was trouble too in Antigua where he was having a house built, I believe, but I think he would of liked to have stayed on with Hampshire if they had been less demanding. However, since they were paying him a healthy salary they felt entitled to ask him to earn it. Like Richards, a parting of the ways was inevitable. Two down and just me to go. The whispers got around that I was the next on my way. This annoyed me because nothing could have been further from the truth, but let me say here and now, there was an unpleasant atmosphere in the Hampshire dressing room which did nothing for my peace of mind.

The whole atmosphere on the county circuit had changed for the worse as a result of the Packer situation. Perhaps we WSC men were expecting too much if we thought it would all be the same on our return. This made our dressing room, for one, a decidely

166

unpleasant place in which to be. It was all decidedly cold and there was a lot of malicious whispering behind our backs from people we had come to regard as friends. Our colleagues spoke to us openly enough but not with any great warmth and it was fairly obvious that our presence, if not resented, was certainly not welcomed. No matter what we did on behalf of Hampshire County Cricket Club on the pitch, it was never enough. Several times I overheard mutterings from colleagues how if one of us had got a fifty, it should have been a century. I have to admit to feeling both baffled and hurt. Barry and Andy noted the same behaviour and I suppose it may have contributed to their decision to opt out for good in mid-season. I was never tempted to do the same and felt that their attitude towards me would change gradually and they would come to accept me again. I could not really see the motives for the sly digs at us and the little gangs of whisperers. What I had done during the winter was really none of their business and as far as they were concerned I might just as well have been undersealing vans at Southampton Airport. This moral stance of theirs was irritating and I never remember any of them ostracising those among us who had been coaching in South Africa in the winter. Was this less reprehensible than playing for Packer? I can only put their attitude down to a form of jealousy and I have little doubt that many of them would have snapped up any Packer offer as eagerly as I did, had it come their way.

This cold feeling was not just confined to Hampshire, who are a fairly amiable bunch of fellows anyway. One or two counties who have some unpleasant characters among them used to mutter and sneer when fielding if I played and missed at a delivery. The sarcastic comments did nothing to upset me and, after listening to the verbal assaults of the Australians for two years, there was not much they could do except harden my attitude and reinforce my determination to punish them by making plenty of runs. If nothing else, though, it did at least show the depth of feeling stirred by Packer's intrusion and how strongly opposed the average county professional was to his unofficial matches some 12,000 miles away.

With Richards and Roberts departing in controversial

circumstances and with rumours about the impending departure of our skipper, Gilliat, it was a season of turmoil at Hampshire and I discovered that more and more was being expected of me. With Richards gone and Gilliat often injured, it was becoming increasingly imperative for me to bat responsibly and not to come out without a big score under my belt. Apart from the dressing-room pressures which I was learning to shrug off, I felt in good order from the start of the 1978 season and in four of my first five matches I scored half centuries. Almost immediately I had noticed that a winter for Packer had made me a better player and this was confirmed when we went down to Hove to play Sussex in the middle of June.

Tony Greig, the villain of the establishment, had been suspended for a few weeks by the authorities for his part in the whole affair and the match against Hampshire was to be his comeback. An ordinary county match was transformed by television cameras and battery of photographers and reporters. A sizeable crowd had also come to witness his return to the game after an enforced absence. Even with Greig's return, Sussex were again desperately weak for our visit and there was a hush of expectancy when Greig made his way out to the wicket, surrounded by a posse of photographers. Within what seemed like seconds he was on his way back to the pavilion, out first ball, caught by Greenidge at slip off Andy Roberts. How ironic could it get: Packer's number one henchman dismissed by two of his fellow WSC players, to leave the establishment and their supporters chuckling with glee. More to the point, Sussex were all out for 77 around lunchtime on the first day and Barry and I had overhauled their total in little more than an hour. At the end of the first day, against some of the most docile bowling that I can remember, I was 166 not out. Trevor Jesty and I went on to make 242 for the the third wicket before I was bowled by John Spencer for 211. Apparently my innings consisted of 7 sixes and 24 fours and I think it was sheer boredom which removed me in the end. Greig fared a little better in the second innings, making 31, but we won by the colossal margin of an innings and 141 runs. Ankle and knee injuries stopped me from

168

making the best of the good start to the season and apart from the occasional 50 and 95 against Gloucestershire at Cheltenham, it was not until we went down to Bournemouth for two matches that I hit a vein of good form and success, the like of which I had never encountered before. As far as the championship was concerned, we were long since out of the reckoning and all we had to hope for was a respectable position in the table. With Richards and Roberts gone and a succession of injuries, we had not had a happy season and it was with a certain amount of relief that we greeted Bournemouth and the impending end to a troubled summer.

At Bournemouth I began a run of success which saw me score 510 runs in six innings. I cannot account for it. I was not trying to prove anything to anyone and the wickets were not especially amenable to the batsmen. What is more, I was not grafting and just played every shot purely from instinct. It all sounds so easy and, in fact, it was. To make those figures more impressive, there was a 9 and a nought among them. Warwickshire were my first victims in a match of no real consequence. We trailed by 79 on the first innings, during which I had made 9. Warwickshire left us 302 to win and although they beat us by 37 runs, I had them worried with a score of 112.

Kent were the next team to visit Bournemouth, needing only a win here to clinch the title. Needless to say, large number of their supporters swelled the gate to quite sizeable proportions by Bournemouth standards. Kent could hardly have made a more impressive start and at 329 for 4, left us much to do. Against Jarvis, Underwood and John Shepherd, I batted with complete assurance to make 136. However we were 93 behind on the first innings and for the rest of the second day of the match, the Kent batsmen ruthlessly consolidated so that they left themselves the entire last day in which to get us out. For our part, a target of 312 seemed unrealistic. After my run of two successive centuries, I was half expecting failure and so were Kent. Kent were banking on me failing at last and the champagne had been ordered. The full complement of Kent bowling tried everything they knew on a wicket which traditionally favours the spinners on the last day,

David Rock and I put on 116 for the first wicket and I was feeling in a great mood.

David Turner and I came together with Kent probably needing only one more breakthrough to ensure victory because there was plenty of time at their disposal. Turner offered solid support and I was playing as soundly and as belligerently as at any time since the Sussex match. Underwood tried everything in his repertoire but we carried the fight to him and suddenly the match started to swing in our favour. Kent's supporters, who had been expecting the formality of a Hampshire defeat, were becoming more sullen and silent as a succession of attacking shots sped to the boundary. By the time I was out I had made 120 but Trevor Jesty and Nigel Cowley carried on where I had left off and took Hampshire to the most unlikely win of the championship season. Kent became more and more lethargic in the field and many of the supporters had long since made for the exits by the time the winning runs were scored with a couple of hours and more to spare. The large number of Fleet Street scribes who had come to witness the climax of the championship season were left instead to record our achievement and it was a few more days before Kent were at last able to open that champagne.

For our final match of the season we moved on to Southampton, where Glamorgan were the visitors. I was caught and bowled without scoring in the first innings but I made up for it in the second innings with another knock in which everything went right. I scored 133 eventually and although Glamorgan did their best to chase a large total, we won by 59 runs, thus elevating us somewhat surprisingly to eighth position. My sequence of scores was therefore 9, 112, 136, 120, 0 and 133, giving me an average of 85. The Glamorgan match earned me the Lawrence Trophy for the season's fastest century. The record books say it came in 82 minutes, beating the previous best by nine minutes. What a way to end the season.

The tail-end to the season was made all the more memorable because out of a summer of almost continual problems, we won the John Player League, for the second time, on the last day of the season. My major contribution until the last day down at

Bournemouth was to score 116 against Yorkshire at Portsmouth. It was my first JPL ton for three years, which is not as remarkable as it sounds because a match based on 40 overs each makes a century feasible only if the batsman attacks successfully from the start. Even without Richards and Roberts we kept winning more of these Sunday matches than we lost and, on the final day of the JPL season, three teams had good chances of winning the title. Somerset, who had never won a trophy in a hundred years and more of trying, had a great chance of winning two in the same weekend. But they lost the Gillette Cup final to the underdogs, Sussex, and went back to Taunton to play Essex obviously disheartened by what had happened at Lords. Somerset needed only to win their match to be sure of clinching the JPL as compensation, while Leicestershire, like us, had to win their match to even stand an outside chance. We were playing Brearley's Middlesex at Dean Park where a large crowd had been queueing to get in since early morning. We batted first and against an attack consisting of Daniel, Selvey, Edmonds, Emburey, Gatting (all Test players) and Norman Featherstone, Gilliat and I put on 100 for the first wicket before Gilliat was out for 35. I took the attack to pieces that day to the delight of many people who had crowded into the ground and, with Jesty, put on 120 for the third wicket. Eventually I was caught in the deep for 122 but by then Middlesex were left with the task of scoring at $5\frac{1}{2}$ an over to beat us and to deny us at least a possible share of the title. The news kept filtering through from the other grounds and the word soon got around that Leicestershire had won and that Somerset had dismissed Essex comparatively cheaply.

With the crowd hushed by the news of these setbacks, Radley and Featherstone put on 77 for the first wicket and it seemed as if all the mathematical permutations would be made unnecessary anyway. At 145 for 2 chasing 222, most of our supporters had given up hope, since Middlesex were grafting their way to victory. Then Jesty induced an incredible collapse with 5 for 32 and when the last wicket fell, they were still 26 runs short of beating us. Apparently we had scored our runs quicker than Leicestershire over the season so, although we had the same number of points, we finished higher. This left us about half an hour to fight our way through the crowds and huddle around a television set to watch the last tense minutes of the match at Taunton. Somerset's nerve was giving way and in the desperate search for runs, wickets were being sacrificed needlessly. With every man on the boundary something like four were needed off the last ball of the match and if the atmosphere was electric at Taunton, it was even worse for us glued to the television. Somerset managed only two off the last ball with the wicketkeeper running with the ball from near the boundary to deny the home team the precious runs they craved so despairingly. We were the champions and the little dressing room at Bournemouth erupted in a deafening roar of delight. The crowd, who had waited patiently for up to half an hour, joined in the sheer ecstasy of triumph. Each one of us was called by the many people who had stayed to cheer, to take a bow and to acknowledge their continual chanting. The drinks flowed again that night and the bitterness, disappointments and the problems of a chaotic and unhappy season were forgotten in a torrent of hastily summoned champagne. Never did bubbly taste sweeter.

Having successfully negotiated a troublesome English summer and won back those supporters who had disowned me, I had little time to relax before Packer called again. New players had been signed and it looked as if the competition would be all the tougher because of it. I had time only to collect again the award for the greatest number of sixes in an English season before jetting to Australia. WSC had increased the prize money and with the floodlighting improved, everything was ready for another hard three months.

The West Indians got off to a slow start and we lost some early matches without making much of a contribution. Kerry Packer, a hard and arrogant man in my estimation, was furious about our poor beginning because his organisation were just starting to win over the Australian public to such an extent that attendances were better than for the official England–Australia series. Packer called a meeting of the West Indian players and, when we were all assembled, told us to improve in no uncertain terms. He seemed to think we were deliberately shirking after winning the previous year and he promised drastic action unless we pulled ourselves together. I think his remarks showed how little he really understood about the game. We might not have been playing particularly well by our standards but it was grossly unfair to many highly talented opponents to suggest that we were not doing as well as we could simply because we did not feel like it. Nothing could have been further from the truth and in many ways, the success of 1977–8 had rebounded on us. A score of 58 not out was the best I could manage on a revamped and streamlined schedule in the Third Supertest at Melbourne but in the Supertest final at Sydney we lost to the Australians by 10 wickets and left it to the World XI to contest the Supertest Grand Final. It was not a very good year for the West Indians.

I was altogether more successful in the International Cup series, finishing top of the West Indian averages with 478 runs at average of nearly 40. We won the International Cup by virtue of a superior run rate after the Australians had been misled into believing that in fact they had won.

Packer's organisation, heartened by the growing acceptance of the Australian public, decided to try their luck in the West Indies where there was a deep-rooted support for WSC and all it stood for. After the 1978 series when Bobby Simpson captained an under-strength official Australian side against a West Indian team devoid of its stars, the fans in the Caribbean were looking forward eagerly to seeing the best players from both sides in action, and with it the chance of revenge for the humiliations of 1975–6. For the players it meant five more Supertests, twelve one-day matches and enough island-hopping to satisfy the most ardent traveller. We expected it to be gruelling and packed with incident and it was. Two of the Tests were interrupted by riots and one of them—the second at Bridgetown—was abandoned for precisely that reason. It was not a particularly happy series. The schedule was tight and after a season in Australia, it was asking a bit much of us to be at our best. Thomson was reunited with Lillee after his dispute with the Australian Board of Control had been settled, but a mixture of riot

173

and rain prevented their partnership from developing. Australia were crushed by 369 runs in the first of the Supertests in Jamaica; the second in Barbados was destroyed by the rioting and in the third at Port of Spain, we lost by 24 runs. In Guyana there was more crowd trouble and the match was drawn and there was another inconclusive result in the fifth at St John's in Antigua. My own part in all this was a couple of fifties, but with so much good bowling on both sides, there were only glimpses of good batting.

The cricket itself may have been a little disappointing considering so many good players were taking part, but the size of the crowds showed the Packer players and officials that there was support for their type of cricket in the West Indies. It may not have been a particularly successful tour and the ever-increasing threat of riots was a constant worry, but it proved that WSC was acceptable to the West Indian supporters, which in itself was a minor victory over the establishment.

Heading back to England there seemed no way that Packer would back down now having endured so much in the previous two years. After a disjointed and disappointing start it had blossomed with experience and the second year was far better organised and more successful. It came as something of a shock to me, and I am sure many of my WSC colleagues, when it was announced that having acquired the television rights for conventional Tests in Australia, the big top was coming down on the circus. I will go so far as to say I was deeply hurt when the news came through from Australia that this revolutionary set-up was coming to a halt just when it looked set to become as much an acceptable institution as anything the authorities could offer. Cynically I could say that my wallet will be hurt most deeply by Packer's disappearance and there is no doubt about how much I will miss the kind of pay cheques he was giving in return for our services. I would be a liar if I was to say it did not matter. However, it is not just the money that will be missed. Packer's cricket brought a whole new dimension to the game, a whole new concept. I am sure floodlights, white balls, circles on the field, coloured clothing and other such innovations will be seen only as cheap gimmicks by those who abhorred his commercial intrusion into what some may have seen as a gentle game.

As a player, all these ideas took some getting used to. But it was the players who mattered and I never heard of one who openly disliked anything dreamt up by Packer's entourage. There was nothing contrived in the cricket, least of all the finishes, in spite of claims of 'fixes' by our critics. I owe Packer and his cricket a debt of gratitude. Not only did he pay me properly for being a top sportsman, but as a cricketer I felt I improved tremendously. I ceased to become one of the West Indians' 'Happy Hookers', the sort of crowd-pleasers who pleased the Australian crowds even more by giving away their wickets with irresponsible shots. The standard of bowling and fielding was high and the competition unremittingly severe. For those reasons I had to learn to concentrate more and to be prepared to graft patiently when required. I hope I have lost none of my fierceness and my desire to punish every ball is still with me, but now I am more selective about which deliveries I try to hit out of the ground. Irresponsible batting, especially the hook shot, was one of the causes of my pathetic failures on my first Australian tour. I came away from that tour thinking I might not ever become a world-class player. Now, after constant exposure to the very best in bowling, I like to think that the same bowlers at least respect me and hopefully actually fear my batting prowess. My entire approach to the game has changed as a result of WSC and for that I can only thank Packer and his much-maligned pirate series. Some players with vaunted talents were conspicuously failures when subjected to WSC and there were some badly dented reputations along the way. Others, like Garth Le Roux, were shot to prominence. If nothing else it woke up the authorities to the plight of the world's top cricketers and I believe it made them realise just how badly we had been treated, particularly financially, over the years. Now England's players are earning £10,000 for a tour. Would they have been getting that without Kerry Packer?

175

14 Return to the Fold

Cricket was still in a state of turmoil when the World Cup of 1979 was being played. Once more, the West Indies were made firm favourites by the bookmakers and we had reasons to believe that our potential opposition was not as strong as when we first won the Prudential Cup back in 1975. The West Indies, defying pressure from the top, chose their best side which meant that the Packer players formed the majority of the 14 man squad. Eight of the party had been members of the last trophy-winning squad so that we had both talent and, importantly, vital experience to help our cause. Australia, our greatest rivals over recent years, were steadfastly refusing to use any of their Packer players and were parading what amounted to their third best side again. To add to their troubles, many of the young Australians had had little real experience of limited-over cricket and there was no doubt that qualifying for the semi-finals would be something of an achievement in itself for them. We saw Pakistan and England as our major rivals. Pakistan, as in 1975, had enough brilliant strokemakers to beat any team on their day but temperament, individual and collective, had let them down in the past and could do so again at any time. England, with Australia, Pakistan and Canada in their group had plenty of knowledge of the overs-limit game and, in front of their own crowds, were bound to pose a problem. In our group were New Zealand, Sri Lanka and India and it would have been a national disaster if we had failed to reach the semi-finals in the company of such teams. Not surprisingly, there was a mood of great optimism among the West Indians but, if truth were known, we would rather have played against the best players from each country for such a prestigious trophy, won four years ago in such exciting circumstances.

The West Indian party was Clive Lloyd, Farroud Bacchus, Colin Croft, Joel Garner, Larry Gomes, Gordon Greenidge, Desmond Haynes, Michael Holding, Alvin Kallicharran, Collis King, Malcolm Marshall, Deryck Murray, Viv Richards and Andy Roberts. As far as I was concerned, the second World Cup gave me an opportunity to make up for the personal failures of the first. Apart from one fifty in the semi-final, I had not done myself justice and after four years of continual cricket, I felt I was a vastly improved player from the one who batted so tentatively against the Australian quick bowlers in the Lords final. Three big Test series and two winters with Packer had, in my opinion, made me a much more responsible batsman and I was determined not to let this chance to right a few wrongs pass me by.

Our first match was against India at Edgbaston, where they were sure of almost as much support as ourselves from the immigrant communities. India have plenty of magnificent batsmen, of course, but adventure is not one of their strong points and with a limited bowling line-up, they were not expected to cause us many problems. So it proved. Viswanath battled gamely and intelligently to make 75 but a total of 190 was not designed to halt our progress. With only Kapil Dev approaching anything more than medium pace, Haynes and I plundered runs at will and we put on 138 for the first wicket. By the time Desmond was out, the match was as good as won and it really became a case of whether I could reach my century before the winning runs were scored. I am pleased to say that I made 106 not out in our 9 wicket win and was duly named man-of-the-match for my contribution to a crushing victory. Sri Lanka were our next scheduled opponents and they came away with the distinction of having taken two points from us.

The match was to have been played at the Oval and I think it fair to say that Sri Lanka were expecting a fair old hiding from us, especially after our confidence-boosting win over India. For three days we waited for the rain to stop to give us a chance to get out and play. Every day the prospects were as gloomy as ever and in the end it was abandoned without a ball being bowled and each side collected a couple of points. The Sri Lankans were delighted. They would rather have played us, of course, and faced the consequences, but there were one or two broad smiles in their dressing room when it was called off. New Zealand, who are underrated because they underrate themselves, had plenty of experienced ability at their disposal and we were not going to take them lightly. Our caution was justified by their early results. They had beaten Sri Lanka by 9 wickets and India equally emphatically by 8. This put them above us in the group table when we came to meet them at Trent Bridge in the last match before the semi-finals. Both teams were already certain to qualify. Predictably, New Zealand made it hard for us. We batted first and I felt in no great danger against the belligerence of Richard Hadlee or anyone else at their disposal. We always managed to score at something like 4 an over and I was disappointed when I edged the gentle bowling of Coney to Bruce Edgar because, with 65 to my name, there was no earthly reason why I could not have gone on and got another ton. Clive Lloyd carried on the good work and was unbeaten with 73 when our overs ran out with the West Indies at 244 for 7. It was asking much of the solid New Zealand batting to keep going at more than 4 an over against our bowlers. But how they fought. Wickets fell too often to put the issue in doubt but Hadlee showed his versatility with a brave 42 before time overtook them and we won by 32 runs. This put us in the semi-finals against Pakistan, who were sure to provide us with our sternest test so far.

Pakistan had been runners-up in Group B and after losing to England were forced to face us at the Oval in the semi-final. I am not sure if we would have preferred England or Pakistan at this stage of the competition because the semi-finals tend to be a test of nerve as much as skill and luck can play a crucial part. The Oval was packed as we had expected with big faction of support for both sides. We batted first and I was both confident and eager to get under way. Imran was bowling quite fast but too short while Sarfraz could do little right. Haynes and I got off to a solid start, accelerating when possible and punishing a fair number of bad deliveries. I had made 73 with the minimum of trouble in 30 overs when the occasional bowling of Asif Iqbal induced me to touch a catch to the wicketkeeper. By this time we had made 132 and the damage had been done. Haynes went on to score 65 and with just about all our major batsmen taking advantage of a nice batting wicket, our total of 293 for six would normally have been enough to see us through to the final.

However, we were well aware how good the Pakistani batting could be if it suited them, in which case they had the potential to overhaul such a score comparatively easily. Sadiq was soon out, but standing at second slip I put down a catch from Majid who had then scored only 10. My lapse began to look expensive as Majid and Zaheer, two fine attacking batsmen, piled on 166 for the second wicket. Colin Croft then removed both inside 11 runs and my relief must almost have been audible to spectators in the back row of the stands. Gradually their resistance faltered and at something like 8.10 on a bright summer's evening, the last of their wickets fell still 44 runs short or victory. Since Zaheer had made 93, Majid 81 and there had been a lot of good, restrictive bowling, the candidates for man of the match were many and adjudicator John Edrich was faced with a difficult task in choosing one. I was surprised and delighted when, in some controversy, he chose me for having done so much in getting the West Indies off to a decisively fast start. This meant that in two of the three matches in which we had played I had been nominated man of the match and I went into the Lords final with an average of 122 in the World Cup matches. England beat New Zealand's brave challenge by 9 runs in the other semi-final at Old Trafford and somewhat predictably ensured a England–West Indies confrontation in the final, the match everyone wanted.

Lords was full again and there was an air of expectancy every bit as potent as the same day in 1975 as Haynes and I went out to bat first. I have to admit that I was not at my best in those opening overs and I had made only 9 from as many overs when I went for a suicidal run after pushing the ball out towards Derek Randall. I paid the penalty for taking liberties with one of the world's finest fielders. England bowled intelligently and with some success in the

179

morning session and it needed an explosive partnership of 139 in 21 overs by Richards and King to lift us out of some unexpected trouble. Richards was 138 not out when we ran out of time and the feeling was that with our array of fast bowlers, England would never get anywhere near 287 unless someone in the middle order really accelerated. Their target was under 5 an over, which was by no means impossible. Brearley and Boycott bravely took the sting from our opening flurry of fast-bowling activity and the runs started to mount disconcertingly. I can reveal that we were beginning to worry as the total neared 100 and we had still not taken a wicket. If Brearley and Boycott had been more ambitious and adventurous, the outcome of the whole match might have been different. They failed to realise that we were rattled and disheartened by our inability to part them. More positive strikers of the ball would have beaten us but the England opening pair failed to take advantage of their own good sense, our indifferent bowling and an increasing number of fielding mistakes. Our conferences at the end of each over became more urgent as the runs continued to be scored. Eventually we came to the conclusion that although Brearley and Boycott were firmly in control, they were not making their runs quickly enough and we resolved to keep them in. It may have seemed an unusually negative tactic for the West Indians to adopt but it appeared to be the best course of action.

The pair were not parted until the score had reached 129 and, on paper, it looked as if they had done a good job. In a way, they had. But it had taken them 38 overs to accumulate their runs and had thrust a terrible responsibility on the men deputed to follow them. This may sound a little unfair, but the Boycott–Brearley partnership was as much responsible for our ultimate victory as anything we did ourselves. Joel Garner took 5 wickets in 11 balls later on an England went from 183 for 3 to 194 all out in four overs. Wickets were lost trying to make up lost time and with Viv named man of the match, we were home and dry by the significantly large margin of 92 runs.

The celebrations were every bit as hectic as when we had first won the Prudential World Cup four years before and, although we had been red-hot favourites, we had been forced to work hard to justify the bookies' odds. The champagne tasted that much sweeter for me because the World Cup had been an unprecedented personal success. My aggregate of 253 runs at an average of more than 84 was outstanding and might have been better but for the stupid run-out in the final. In fact I scored more runs than any other player in the 1979 World Cup and that in itself is an achievement of which I shall be proud always.

From the glory and the hysteria of a World Cup final at Lords it was back to earth with a bump on my return to county duty with Hampshire. Without Richards, Roberts and Gilliat, all of whom had left county cricket, the team had been struggling. New skipper Bob Stephenson had been given a difficult task leading an inexperienced side and Hampshire had suffered a humiliating run of defeats. It was not a good time to return. The best we could hope for was a respectable position in the championship table and with early elimination from both the Benson and Hedges Cup and the Gillette Cup, there was not even the solace of success in the John Player League, of which we were champions. I won the man-of-the-match award against Middlesex at Lords in the Gillette Cup with a score of 87 in a match we dominated and yet somehow contrived to lose, but for many of us it was a disappointing domestic season. My aggregate of 1,404 championship runs at an average of just over 50 showed that I had done my best for Hampshire but collectively we were a weak outfit and, as far as I am concerned, the season was memorable only for one exceptional innings. We were playing Warwickshire in a JPL match at Edgbaston and with 10 sixes and 13 fours, scored 163 not out in a match we won only narrowly. It was scored off 120 deliveries and became the highest individual total in a John Player League match. It was also the most sixes made in one JPL innings and gave me the record number of sixes in the history of the JPL. The innings at Edgbaston gave me a unique position in county cricket because it meant that I held the batting records in all three one-day competitions at the same time. Warwickshire had neither Bob Willis nor David Brown and so the bowling was easily overwhelmed. Like all my batting records, I was unaware of it until somebody told me afterwards. I have never chased records but, once achieved, they are jealously guarded.

Curiously enough, the previous highest score in the John Player League was 155 by Barry Richards against Yorkshire—at least the record stays within the county. Those 10 sixes at Edgbaston enabled me to win the six-hitting award again. It is always nice to think that over a whole season, no one has hit the ball over the top of the boundary more times than me. Thanks to my stint with Packer and to the realisation that Hampshire needed my experience, I batted far more responsibly than I can ever remember and so it came as something of a surprise to discover that I had won the six-hitting award once more. For the rest, I shall draw a veil over the summer; it was a bit of a disappointment for us at Hampshire.

The news of Packer's demise was, as I say, something of a blow and we were all left to wonder what sort of series was being prepared for us for the winter of 1979–80 as international cricket strove to return to normal after two years of acrimony and chaos. I had been playing cricket continuously for something like eight years but I was looking forward to returning to Australia for another tough round of one-day internationals and three Test matches. I never get tired of playing cricket. As a professional, who has earned a good living from the game, I like to be involved all the time and the prospect of playing the Aussies yet again was something of a compensation after the loss of WSC.

With Anita and Carl in Australia to watch me, the winter was both enjoyable and rewarding. After a poor start, the West Indies recovered to reach the World Series Cup finals where we overcame England, the other team who know how to play limited-overs cricket, in two interesting matches during which I made 80 and 98 not out. Those innings were enough to earn me a special award for Player of the Finals. It also gave me a gold medallion and a bonus of 2,000 dollars.

Our schedule was a tough one with constant travelling and matches being played at what seemed like all hours of the day and night. Many of my better scores in the one-day matches were

182

scored under floodlights with the aid of a white ball. England were obviously at a disadvantage having never played under lights before and I only hope they found the novelty as exciting as the majority of men who had played under them for WSC. With the two big scores in the finals, I hope I finally dispelled lingering beliefs that my big scores only came in matches which did not matter. We in the West Indies camp take great pride of our tag of world champions and, having twice won the World Cup, were equally keen to become the first holders of the newly created World Series Cup. Based over something like eleven matches on grounds and pitches of contrasting calibre, it was never going to be easy, especially as Australia were at full strength for the first time in a couple of years. Perhaps it was a surprise and certainly a disappointment to the Australian cricketing public that the home side did not do better in the one-day matches but I believe the greater experience of the West Indians and England was too much in the end.

It was the first time the West Indians had been back to Australia for a legitimate Test series since that terrible winter of discontent in 1975–6 and there was not a player among us who did not wish to erase the memory of the disasters of the 5–1 setbacks. Nine of our sixteen-man squad had been on that tour and we soon impressed it upon the newcomers the importance of getting a measure of revenge. Larry Gomes, Malcolm Marshall and Derek Parry were all playing in Australia for the first time but there was only about three weeks in which to build up to the Frist Test at Brisbane.

I warmed up with scores of 45 and 9 against South Australia and a couple of 20s against an Invitation XI. These were largely preliminaries for the one-day matches and we went into the First Test having just lost to England in a rain-affected match at Sydney. At Brisbane Viv Richards was again outstanding, although he had been complaining about a groin injury for some time. Bruce Laird (92) and Greg Chappell (74) helped Australia reach 268 and it was our turn to bat. Brisbane's 'Gabba ground was, of course, the scene of my disastrous 'pair' and I would not have been human had I not thought back to that match. Could it all happen again?

I can tell you, there was no happier man than me in Brisbane when I got off the mark. Jeff Thomson gave me a piece of luck when he dropped me off a skier when I was still in single figures and I was quite pleased to have gone on and made 34. Dennis Lillee, my oldest and most successful adversary, was responsible for my dismissal with a catch behind the wicket, but with Richards (140), Rowe (50) and Garner scoring 60 we were 173 ahead on the first innings. Greg Chappell, Laird and Kim Hughes saw Australia to safety and I promptly returned to my 'Brisbane form' with a second innings nought in a tame draw.

My form in the one-day matches was altogether better and just before the Second Test against the Australians, Viv Richards and I each scored 85 not out in a 9 wicket cup win over England. And so to the MCG for another chance at claiming revenge. With two Tests to go, victory at Melbourne would have provided an important psychological boost for whichever side won. Michael Holding took four cheap wickets and Australia were in real trouble on the first day at all out for 156. We were adamant that we were not going to let this opportunity slip.

Desmond Haynes was an early casualty but Viv Richards and I broke the back of the Australian resistance with a big second-wicket partnership and I should have done better when, having scored 48 and looking secure and settled, offered a relatively gentle catch to mid-on. The West Indies were pleased enough with my contribution and Viv went on to make 96 and Roberts 54 as Australia toiled in vain. We were out in the end for 397 and we were sure that this time our opponents were not going to escape as they had done at Brisbane. Laird and Hughes defied us gamely with half centuries but we needed only 19 to go one up in the series and it gave me great pleasure to be at the crease when the winning runs were scored. Ten wickets could scarcely have provided a more convincing margin of victory and the best the Australians could now hope for was to level the series. At Adelaide, of course, they failed and no one can now dispute our claim to be the best team in the world.

The WSC finals provided me with my greatest personal

moments of the whole tour and it was deeply gratifying to hear both England captain Mike Brearley and Lloyd himself pay tribute to me in public. It made all the struggles of the past seem worthwhile and confirmed the belief that I was now not simply a Test cricketer of some ability, but a world-class cricketer. At moments like this it seems strange to recall how Hampshire nearly sacked me—and not without valid reasons—and the efforts I had made to turn myself into an acceptable cricketer, good enough to play at county level. Only ten years ago I was new to the Hampshire staff and thinking of quitting an underpaid job for something worthwhile. Now the tears and the tribulations have paid off and I aim to stay at the top for as long as possible, certainly for another five or six years, injuries permitting.

While I am in reflective mood, it is a pleasant exercise to think back to all the players I have played with or against over the years and to choose what I consider the perfect team. Every fan and critic has their own idea of a World XI and I am not saying for one moment that these are categorically the best players in the world. All I am saying is that these are the men who I consider would represent the best balanced outfit and would give any other XI a tough match. The Gordon Greenidge Superteam would read (in batting order):

1 Sunil Gavaskar
2 Roy Fredericks
3 Viv Richards
4 Greg Chappell (captain)
5 Alvin Kallicharran
6 Imran Khan
7 Alan Knott/Rod Marsh
8 Ian Botham
9 Mike Holding
10 Dennis Lillee
11 Derek Underwood

There are obviously going to be howls of protest from people who say: 'But what about so-and-so ?' Let me, then, explain my choice. First of all, there may seem to be a bias towards West Indian players. This is not because I am so one-eyed that I cannot see players from other teams. You have heard my views on West Indian cricket and you will realise that, if anything, the bias is in the other direction. My aim was simply to pick the best players available, preferably if they are still playing the game.

In my opinion, Sunil Gavaskar of India is the most consistent opening batsman in the Test arena. By the turn of 1980 he had scored 23 Test centuries which, for a man who is by no means a veteran, is a phenomenal performance. Packer did him a disservice by not signing him because he might then have blossomed and received the acclaim he deserves. As an opening batsman, I know what an onerous task it is to face the new ball and fresh, hostile bowlers. It requires nerve, skill and an iron will. Gavaskar has all of these qualities and his incredible consistency will one day earn him a place among the game's greats. Gavaskar may not have the panache of my old colleague, Barry Richards, for instance, but in the end a batsman is judged on what he actually achieves and, for a relatively young man, Gavaskar has already achieved a tremendous amount. His rivals for that particular job I thought would be Geoff Boycott and Ian Redpath, two very difficult customers to get out. Both have this habit of occupying the crease with unwavering concentration and steadily accumulating runs and their respective records show how successful they have been. Redpath was our main obstacle during the 1975–6 tour but hardly looked a cricketer with his skinny frame and sloping shoulders. Yet how fantastically successful he was against us. He was the man who broke our resistance with his sheer obduracy. Boycott's strengths and weaknesses have been well documented and I do not think he will ever live down his absence when England were at their weakest in the mid-70s. No man who scores a century of centuries can be described as lacking in any way. There was and, I think still is, a suspicion about Boycott against genuinely fast bowling. Many such doubts might have disappeared after his triumphs in Australia in the winter of 1979–80 but Lillee hardly ever bowled at his fastest and in the previous winter the pace of Rodney Hogg produced the suspicion that it was too much for him on occasions.

Let me say now that no one likes facing genuinely fast bowling. It is a question of how well the batsman adjusts to the demands and some play it better than others. There is a split second to get in line and to play the shot and I would have liked to have seen Boycott against the world's fast bowlers when they were in their prime.

The other opening position in my team goes to Roy Fredericks. Roy and I may not have been the closest of friends but I have great respect for his sharp reflexes and his ability to hit the ball hard. For an opening batsman, these are tremendous qualities and I put him ahead of Barry because of his penchant for immediate attack. The man to partner Gavaskar must be able to score quickly and Fredericks can do just that.

The middle-order men virtually pick themselves. Viv Richards has developed into a truly magnificent player with the full range of attacking shots—not all of them out of the textbook—and he can destroy any bowling line-up in world cricket. Viv's record is his greatest testimonial and he is so good that he can take outrageous chances and get away with them and in the process demoralise good-class bowlers. As I said earlier, there is no rivalry between Viv and me. We have a great mutual respect and I am always glad when he is playing for us and not against us, as he does for Somerset. At times it is almost impossible to bowl to him and there are not many players in Test cricket about whom that can be said. Zaheer Abbas might be considered for one of the middle-order places. His flamboyant cover drives make him a majestic player to watch and on good wickets a murderer of any attack. On poorer wickets, Zaheer has his faults and for that reason I leave him out. No such thing could be said about my number four and captain, Greg Chappell.

Greg does everything on a cricket field so well. His batting is impeccable, his technique flawless and there is not a shot he cannot play. As a captain he is an astute reader of the game, possibly not as cunning as his brother, Ian, but also a handy change bowler, capable of taking wickets when required. David Hookes is a player I admire and one day he will develop into an outstanding batsman as will David Gower, but I believe that neither seriously rival Alvin Kallicharran for the number five job. Alvin is a little underrated but over the years he has become a tremendously valuable member of the West Indian team. His technique is so tight and correct and he is always prepared to attack when the occasion demands. A fine little player.

Imran Khan may cause a few raised eyebrows among people who do not consider him to be quite in the category of world class. I believe him to be a real asset as an all-rounder and he has the basic ability to develop into a great player. He sometimes chooses the wrong ball to attack and he has a tendency to bowl too short at times, but there is no mistaking his quality nor his talent. Ian Botham comes into this team at number eight, which is his best position at the moment, though he too can become a great all-rounder, capable of batting higher in the order. Ian's greatest characteristic is his competitiveness, his desire to excel. England have been a bit short of these sorts of men lately and there is no his ability to swing the ball in certain conditions and his never-flagging stamina, he is already a fine bowler. His batting will get better when he learns to be more judicious.

In front of Botham in the order I would have either Alan Knott or Rodney Marsh as the wicketkeeper. Much thought has still not resolved which of the two I prefer. Both are excellent wicketkeepers and batsmen with enough talent to have made more than one Test century. I find it absolutely impossible to split them and so I have taken the coward's way out and selected them both. Deryck Murray must be mentioned because he is a capable batsman and by no means a bad wicketkeeper. However, I do not think he quite ranks with Knott and Marsh.

The two finest quick bowlers in the world are Dennis Lillee and Michael Holding. Say what you like about the others—Thomson, Hogg, Roberts, Croft, Procter, Le Roux, Garner—these two are way out in front in my opinion. Three or four years ago Proctor would have merited very close consideration and Roberts and Thomson have both stood the test of time. Holding is the fastest of the lot, believe you me. He is also extremely accurate and with his lightning speed in the field and his great agility, he is a marvellous asset to any side. As for Lillee, all I can say is that I have never been happy nor comfortable against him for long. He may have slowed a little but if he stays clear of injury, will go on and test the best with his clever use of the ball, his refusal to give up and his sheer craftiness. When required, he can also bowl as fast as at any time in his career for short spells and I believe a new ball attack of Lillee and Holding would be too much for any batsman eventually. With Derek Underwood as my spinner that, then, is the Greenidge XI and I only wish I could play in it. I hope I have not offended anyone by leaving them out, but no offence is intended to anyone, least of all Clive Lloyd, whose name I could find no place for.

So much for the present and the past; what of the future? Without conceit, I think I can say that I am at the top of my profession and I hope to stay there for a few more years. With luck, there will be a few more years of Test competition to occupy me and I shall be happy to continue my county career when all that comes to an end.

I don't see myself going on much beyond my middle thirties, though I have had so much enjoyment out of the game I dare say I shall go on until it is no longer physically possible to play. There is the possible prospect of a benefit season looming at Hampshire as recognition for service with the club. When it is all over, I would like to stay in the game in some capacity, maybe as a coach somewhere. It would be hard, not to say impossible, to break away from cricket completely. The game has given me a pleasant living in recent years and enabled me to see the world and to meet many nice people. My dream is to return to the West Indies, to Barbados eventually, to where it all began.

When I return depends on the schooling of my son, Carl. I want him to have a sound education because this is something I feel I may have missed. I would be prepared to pay for an education for him so that he was not left the choice which confronted me: 'Be a good cricketer or face years in an unskilled, undemanding job.' I hope Carl does not want to be a cricketer because there are so many other things for him to do when he grows up. But let me say, finally, that I do not regret for one moment my decision to play this great game. It will be a sad day when I am forced to retire and the greatest compliment for which I could wish would be for other people to regret my retirement as well. It has been a privilege to play at the highest level and I can only thank the many people who have helped me make it possible. I dare say that I might have upset one or two people in the course of this book, but my views are honestly held. I dare say, also, that my style of play will have upset the purists. All I can say is, in the words of the song, I did it my way.

Appendix
C. G. Greenidge—
A Statistical Survey

(compiled by Jim Baldwin)

Season-by-season in first-class cricket

Year	Country	M	I	NO	Runs	HS	Average	100s	50s	Ct	Runs	W	Best	Average
						Batting and Fielding							Bowling	
1970	In England	7	11	1	351	73	35·10	—	4	6	0	0	—	—
1971	In England	24	45	2	1164	102	27·06	1	6	13	57	5	5/49	11·40
1972	In England	22	38	1	1230	142	33·24	2	6	10	173	3	1/3	57·66
1972–3	In West Indies	6	12	0	368	88	30·66	—	2	3	25	0	—	—
1973	In England	22	38	4	1656	196*	48·70	5	9	36	36	2	2/20	18·00
1973–4	In West Indies	6	11	2	353	90	39·22	—	2	4	22	0	—	—
1974	In England	22	33	2	1093	273*	35·25	2	6	23	—	—	—	—
1974–5	In India	12	21	2	869	107	45·73	1	7	9	4	0	—	—
1974–5	In Pakistan	1	2	2	40	27	40·00	—	—	—	—	—	—	—
1974–5	In West Indies	1	2	0	14	8	7·00	—	—	—	—	—	—	—
1975	In England	16	27	0	1120	259	41·48	2	4	26	92	5	3/84	18·40
1975–6	In Australia	7	13	0	290	76	22·30	—	3	4	0	0	—	—
1975–6	In West Indies	2	2	0	127	106	63·50	1	—	3	—	—	—	—
1976	In England	20	38	3	1952	134	55·77	8	8	28	—	—	—	—
1976–7	In West Indies	9	17	0	859	136	50·52	2	6	8	—	—	—	—
1977	In England	19	32	3	1771	208	61·06	6	6	18	4	0	—	—
1977–8	In West Indies	2	3	1	131	80*	65·50	—	1	1	—	—	—	—
1978	In England	19	34	1	1771	211	53·66	5	9	34	8	1	1/8	8·00
1978–9	In West Indies	1	1	0	31	31	31·00	—	—	1	10	0	—	—
1979	In England	17	30	2	1404	145	50·14	3	8	27	—	—	—	—
1979–80	In Australia	6	11	1	308	76	30·80	—	1	13	—	—	—	—
TOTAL		241	421	26	16902	273*	42·78	38	88	267	431	16	5/49	23·93

Highest score in first-class cricket
273* for D. H. Robins' XI v Pakistanis (Eastbourne) 1974
Highest score for Hampshire
259 v Sussex (Southampton) 1975

Highest score for Barbados
136 v Jamaica (Montego Bay) 1976–7

Season-by-season in Test cricket

1974-5	v India	5	9	0	371	107	41·22	1	2	5	—	—	—
1975-6	v Australia	2	4	0	11	8	2·75	—	1	1	0	—	—
1976	v England	5	10	1	592	134	65·77	3	2	7	—	—	—
1976-7	v Pakistan	5	10	0	536	100	53·60	1	4	8	—	—	—
1977-8	v Australia	2	3	1	131	80*	65·50	—	1	1	—	—	—
1979-80	v Australia	3	6	1	173	76	34·60	—	1	3	—	—	—
TOTAL		22	42	3	1814	134	46·51	5	10	25	0	—	—

Highest score in Test cricket
134 for West Indies v England (Old Trafford) 1976

First class centuries

Gordon has scored 38 first-class centuries to 1 February 1980

102	Hampshire v Oxford University (Oxford) 1971
124	Hampshire v Essex (Chelmsford) 1972
142	Hampshire v Sussex (Hove) 1972
196*	Hampshire v Yorkshire (Leeds) 1973
109	Hampshire v Somerset (Taunton) 1973
153	Hampshire v Lancashire (Southport) 1973
104	Hampshire v Worcestershire (Worcester) 1973
118	Hampshire v Kent (Southampton) 1973
120	Hampshire v Middlesex (Lords) 1974
273*	D. H. Robins' XI v Pakistanis (Eastbourne) 1974
107	West Indies v India (1st Test) (Bangalore) 1974–5
259	Hampshire v Sussex (Southampton) 1975
168	Hampshire v Worcestershire (Worcester) 1975
106	Barbados v Jamaica (Bridgetown) 1975–6
115	West Indians v Somerset (Taunton) 1976
101*	West Indians v Leicestershire (Leicester) 1976
134	West Indies v England (3rd Test) (Old Trafford) 1976
101	West Indies v England (3rd Test) (Old Trafford) 1976
115	West Indies v England (4th Test) (Leeds) 1976
123	West Indians v Middlesex (Lords) 1976
130	West Indians v Glamorgan (Swansea) 1976
122	West Indians v Nottinghamshire (Nottingham) 1976
136	Barbados v Jamaica (Montego Bay) 1976–7
100	West Indies v Pakistan (5th Test) (Kingston) 1976–7
200*	Hampshire v Surrey (Guildford) 1977
108	Hampshire v Surrey (Bournemouth) 1977
139	Hampshire v Lancashire (Old Trafford) 1977
124	Hampshire v Nottinghamshire (Basingstoke) 1977
208	Hampshire v Yorkshire (Leeds) 1977
143	Hampshire v Gloucestershire (Southampton) 1977
211	Hampshire v Sussex (Hove) 1978
112	Hampshire v Warwickshire (Bournemouth) 1978

136   Hampshire v Kent (Bournemouth) 1978
120   Hampshire v Kent (Bournemouth) 1978
133   Hampshire v Glamorgan (Southampton) 1978
104   Hampshire v Somerset (Taunton) 1979
145   Hampshire v Middlesex (Portsmouth) 1979
118   Hampshire v Surrey (Oval) 1979

Season-by-season in the John Player League

Year	Inn.	NO	Runs	HS	Average	100	50s	6s	Ct	Runs	Wks	Average
			Batting and Fielding							*Bowling*		
1970	4	0	47	23	11·75	—	—	1	1	—	—	—
1971	14	0	309	62	22·07	—	2	4	5	2	0	—
1972	15	2	428	84	32·92	—	4	8	6	83	1	83·00
1973	13	0	329	69	25·31	—	2	3	7	—	—	—
1974	14	0	432	102	30·85	1	2	7	4	—	—	—
1975	13	0	403	102	31·00	1	2	10	2	—	—	—
1976	—	—	—	—	—	—	—	—	—	—	—	—
1977	10	0	377	91	37·70	—	2	13	5	—	—	—
1978	13	0	637	122	49·00	2	4	20	3	—	—	—
1979	14	2	542	163*	45·16	1	2	15	5	—	—	—
TOTAL	110	4	3504	163*	33·05	5	20	81	38	85	1	85·00

Highest score in the John Player League
163*   for Hampshire v Warwickshire (Edgbaston) 1979

Season-by-season in the Gillette Cup

1971	2	0	28	24	14·00	—	—	1	—	—	—
1972	3	0	47	32	15·66	—	—	1	—	—	—
1973	2	0	127	100	63·50	1	—	3	4	0	—
1974	2	0	42	36	21·00	—	—	2	—	—	—
1975	2	0	202	177	101·00	1	—	1	—	—	—
1976	—	—	—	—	—	—	—	—	—	—	—
1977	3	1	188	106*	94·00	1	1	1	—	—	—
1978	1	0	5	5	5·00	—	—	—	—	—	—
1979	2	0	91	87	45·50	—	1	1	—	—	—
TOTAL	17	1	730	177	45·62	3	2	10	4	0	—

Highest score in the Gillette Cup
177 for Hampshire v Glamorgan (Southampton) 1975

Season-by-season in the Benson & Hedges Cup

1972	4	0	170	81	42·50	—	2	—	2	47	0	—
1973	5	1	262	173*	65·50	1	—	1		—	—	—
1974	5	1	122	40	21·66	—	—	2		—	—	—
1975	6	0	212	111	35·33	1	—	3		—	—	—
1976	1	0	37	37	37·00	—	—	—		—	—	—
1977	5	0	191	103	38·20	1	1	4		—	—	—
1978	3	0	123	61	41·00	—	1	1		—	—	—
1979	4	0	58	51	14·50	—	1	1		—	—	—
TOTAL	33	2	1175	173*	37·90	3	5	12		47	0	—

Highest score in the Benson & Hedges Cup
173* for Hampshire v Minor Counties South (Amersham) 1973

Season-by-season in the Prudential World Cup

Year	Inns	NO	Runs	HS	Average	100s	50s	Ct	Runs	Wkts	Average
			Batting and Fielding						*Bowling*		
1975	4	0	88	55	32·00	—	1	—	—	—	—
1979	4	1	253	106*	84·33	1	2	—	—	—	—
TOTAL	8	1	341	106*	48·71	1	3	—	—	—	—

Highest score in the Prudential World Cup

106* for West Indies v India (Edgbaston) 1979

Benson & Hedges World Series Cup (held in Australia)

| 1979–80 | 8 | 2 | 404 | 98* | 67·33 | — | 4 | 3 | — | — | — |

Highest score in the B & H World Series Cup
98* for West Indies v England (Sydney) 1979–80

World Series Cricket (Supertests)

(held in Australia)

1977–8	11	1	428	140	42·80	1	1	3	—	—	—
1978–9	6	1	133	58*	26·60	—	1	5	—	—	—

(In West Indies)

1978–9	6	0	193	58	32·17	—	2	3	—	—	—
TOTAL	23	2	754	140	35·90	1	4	11	—	—	—

Highest score in the Supertests
140 for the World XI v Australians (Gloucester Park, Perth) 1977–8

Index

202

206

Wisden, 150
Wokingham, 11
Wood, Graeme, 70
Woolmer, Bob, 143, 149
Worcestershire, 55, 56, 59, 83, 91, 92, 93, 122
World Cup (1975), 66, 111, 112, 116, 119, 120, 124, 131, 138, 176
World Cup (1979), 176, 177, 179, 180, 181

World Series Cricket, 35, 72, 159, 160, 162, 166, 168, 172, 173, 174, 175, 182, 183, 184
Worrell, Sir Frank, 21

YMCA, Barbados, 50
YMCA, Southampton, 17, 18, 21, 44
Yorkshire, 55, 56, 83, 92, 120, 158, 171, 182

Zaheer Abbas, 179, 187